THIS FELLOW WITH
THE FABULOUS SMILE

This Fellow with the Fabulous Smile

a tribute to

BRENDAN KENNELLY

edited by

ÅKE PERSSON

BLOODAXE BOOKS

ISBN: 1 85224 367 8

First published 1996 by
Bloodaxe Books Ltd,
P.O. Box 1SN,
Newcastle upon Tyne NE99 1SN.

Bloodaxe Books Ltd acknowledges
the financial assistance of Northern Arts.

Cover printing by J. Thomson Colour Printers Ltd, Glasgow.

Printed in Great Britain by
Cromwell Press Ltd, Broughton Gifford, Melksham, Wiltshire.

CONTENTS

ACKNOWLEDGEMENTS

Poems by Brendan Kennelly quoted or referred to in this book can, unless otherwise indicated in the text, be found in the following books: *Cromwell* (1987), *A Time for Voices: Selected Poems 1960-1990* (1990), *The Book of Judas* (1991), *Breathing Spaces: Early Poems* (1992), and *Poetry My Arse* (1995), all published by Bloodaxe Books.

Thanks are due to The Gallery Press for their kind permission to reprint Paula Meehan's 'My Father Perceived as a Vision of St Francis', from *Pillow Talk* (Gallery Press, 1994).

Bono's 'Nothing Compares to You...' was first published in the *Sunday Press* (8 December 1991); reprinted here with kind permission of the author.

Reverend John McCarthy's title, 'The Bold Collegian', is taken from Trevor West's book *The Bold Collegians* (Dublin: Trinity College, 1992).

The photograph of Brendan Kennelly at the Abbey Inn was taken by Kerry Kennelly and first appeared in *Kerry's Eye* (23 April 1992).

I would like to offer my genuine thanks to a number of people without whose advice and assistance this book would have been far more difficult to complete: Maria Luísa Basurko, Theo Dorgan, Catherine FitzPatrick, Geraldine Mangan, Antoinette Quinn, and Trevor West. And, of course, to all the contributors, whose dedication and willingness to observe deadlines are hereby acknowledged.

ÅKE PERSSON

Introduction

Coming to Ireland from Sweden in the latter half of the 1980s, I was asked by a friend if I would like to go and listen to a poet called Brendan Kennelly, whom I had vaguely heard of. 'His readings are something special,' I was told. And my friend was right. Before the event, I was slightly worried. As much as I had a deep interest in all kinds of literature, I also felt somewhat intimidated by poetry, its web of intricate meanings, its deliberate and often pompous obscurities. However, in the course of the reading, and subsequent to it, it did not take me long to realise that Brendan Kennelly was a poet speaking in a different voice, firmly committed to speak against obscurity and prejudice, and for personal, artistic and ideological integrity and freedom. For me, therefore, it feels right and easy to talk about the term Kennellian. As this book of personal essays illustrates, this concept may mean different things to different people, which is as it should be. When I attempt to define it, I constantly come back to Kennelly's ability to transform suffering into a sense of comedy and joy. When listening to his poetry readings and lectures, when reading his poetry, plays and essays, I always get this feeling that I am witnessing and partaking in a process where positions that seemed firmly fixed are being challenged and subverted. Almost all his work moves from one level of awareness to another, constantly insisting on three things in particular: honesty, hope and joy. He is acknowledging the darkness, but he is resisting it, moving from darkness, through darkness, into light. By doing so, he makes us see what we have forgotten.

It would be fair to suggest that there are very few writers who, in their own lifetime, manage to have such an immediate effect on so many people's lives as Brendan Kennelly. As poet, dramatist, professor, critic, teacher, public speaker, media personality, advertiser, artistic encourager, mentor, colleague, brother, human being, he has come to mean an awful lot to very many people, in Ireland and, increasingly, elsewhere. Whether one likes it or not, he is a cultural phenomenon. His writing, and especially his poetry, has to some extent, at least, been commented on over the years. But many other activities in his long and prominent career have not received very much attention. As I see it, it is quite clear why this is so. The significance of many of his activities is difficult, indeed next to impossible, to capture and comment on in a traditionally academic format, since they lend themselves badly to that impersonal category. It is a well-known fact that a critical assessment of a writer has to be detached in the name of "scientific objectivity" in order to be taken seriously by those who decide artistic and literary tastes. But if the increasingly influential discipline of Cultural Studies, for example, or sociology, or literary sociology, teaches us anything, it is that cultural expressions and meaning, in this case a writer's reputation and impact, are formed on a wide variety of levels, some of which are often extremely difficult to pinpoint. If, in addition to this, that particular writer's private persona and charisma, on the one hand, and his public persona, on the other, are closely interlinked, the situation becomes even more complex, as it moves far beyond, and far deeper than, the text on the page. After having spent a considerable number of years in Dublin doing research on Kennelly for a doctorate, it became clear to me that a personal approach would move in the direction of adequately reflecting and explaining his wide-ranging influence and enormous popularity.

So, that is what this book is all about. Through personal responses from a broad range of contributors this book helps to explain and offer an understanding of the appeal of the cultural presence which is Brendan Kennelly, while at the same time highlighting his multi-faceted contribution to Irish life. In that sense, this book is a celebration of an impressive and fascinating achievement, as any book on a writer or cultural personality is by definition a celebration of that writer or personality.

However, in my opinion, this book is also a social document, since it explicitly and implicitly deals with and touches on a variety of institutions and issues on the social arena, including the "institution" of Brendan Kennelly himself. As can be seen, attempts have been made to include contributors from many walks of life, young and not so young, well-known and not so well-known, women and men. Many of them have in one way or another worked with Brendan Kennelly on a professional level; some on a more informal level; some know him personally; some do not, they just know of him, a few from a considerable distance. What they all have in common is that they have offered their personal responses to and perspectives on him. I do not wish to spoil the reader's experience in any way by commenting on them or analysing them. What I *can* say is that these responses and perspectives are full of insights, they are moving, serious, emotional, anecdotal, generous, formal, short, long, poetic, direct, revealing, critical, funny. Very much like Brendan Kennelly, himself, you might say, the man, the writer, the cultural force.

Nothing Compares to You...

Why do we not want our poets to do Toyota commercials? Think straight. Why do we not want our poets to have day jobs, to make money, to play happy families? Is there something in us that demands our writers die for and in their own words? Is the price of our immortal praise that they hang from a cross of their choice? Drugs? Alcohol? Exile? As close to the age of 33 as possible?

Some time ago, I was in Paris doing some work and by complete coincidence I found myself in the hotel where Oscar Wilde (swollen with syphilitic gases) exploded all over his room. 'I'm dying beyond my means,' he had said. 'My wallpaper and I are fighting a duel to the death. One or the other of us has to go.' They both went.

Irish writers seem programmed for self-destruction, the blood sacrifice is as central a conceit to our literature as it is in our politics. The Jesus Complex. Now Brendan Kennelly is a different kind of fish. Here we get the feeling of a poet who has played with the demons of Irish literature but is stepping back from the edge, looking around, discovering he loves his life too much to live the Myth. In *The Book of Judas*, an epic poem of twelve parts, he rather dismantles it, taking Wilde's idea that 'Man is least himself when he talks in his own person, give him a mask and he will tell you the truth.' He chooses Judas...

> If I can imagine you I may well be you
> Or it may be that you are me...
>
> ('You Can')

The Book of Judas is an epic achievement and as over the top as the subject deserves. This is a poetry as base as heavy metal, as high as the Holy Spirit flies, comic and tragic, from litany to rant, roaring at times, soaring at other times. Like David in the Psalms, like Robert Johnson in the blues, the poet scratches out Screwtape letters to a God who may or may not have abandoned him, and of course to anyone else who is listening. He takes risks, he gets diverted, but whatever the twist, all roads seem to end at the same religious gate, locked tight with the idea that 'things are not what they should be'. His response: 'The best way to serve the age is to betray it' ('Service'), as vivid a tattoo as any rock 'n' roller could ask for.

And what of Kennelly's age, our time? We as Pilate have presided over the death of Marxist/Leninism and the failure to revive the

11

Judaeo-Christian alternative. What's left to betray? Religion as antagonist, that ould crutch of Irish writing, is not enough for someone as smart as Brendan Kennelly. As a rebel, his five smooth stones are kept for much less obvious Goliaths than Catholic guilt or political gridlock. He knows that with less than five years to go, the twentieth century has left Judas/Kennelly with no one to blame... but himself that is.

> If I'd made the world I'd keep my mouth shut too.
> Especially if I'd made me...
>
> ('Deep')

This is not self-loathing. In poems like 'Spirit Fuck' and 'Abraham's Bosom' he is bold, but whether Kennelly fears God or not, he is certainly not afraid to approach HIM. Perhaps that is why he feels so comfortable around his chosen location and his subject's subject matter. If not exactly stained glass windows, he has found in Christianity a parade of colours, a vat of symbolism, ceremonies and rituals that take on new meaning when juxtaposed with the cruel mundanity of the real world: Cork, Dublin, Trinity College... well, nearly the real world. He has, in Irish literary terms, revisited the scene of the crime, remade Jesus in his own image and collated a very different book of evidence. He lets us watch as he stands bowlegged at a crossroads in time and culture, playing stretch with knives of fear and faith, irony and soul, the fist of vision, the hard-nose of reality.

If 'most people ignore most poetry because most poetry ignores most people' (Adrian Mitchell), this is not true of Kennelly's work. He makes his subject accessible:

> Did he ever fish for eels
>   And watch them die at his feet
> Wriggling like love in the dust?
>   Gospels, you're incomplete.
>
> ('My Mind of Questions')

It's not all lyricism. The cardinal reds and royal blues of earlier work harshly contrasted by the dull greys and shit browns of a place we recognise.

The headiness of 'A Dream of Yellow Rain' is balanced by the pink skin pornographic detail of poems like 'Here Is Monica Now' or 'Stains'. He is, thank God, as mesmerised by the ordinary world as the extraordinary things we are doing to it. Even if his 'lips' betray him:

> When I see trout flashing through water
> They close in wonder.
> When my blood is chill with anger
> They are po-faced diplomats.

When I see pictures that make heaven a possibility
They ooze platitudes like spittle.
When I see precision bombers at work
They suck horror like mother's milk.
('Lips')

Over eight years the pilgrim progresses through 400 poems (I heard there were 800), only occasionally crossing the borders of embarrassment in a medium frequently even more indulgent than rock and roll.

An academic, he has broken his own code of class reference, the pratspeak that throws a ring around poetry and that I might have to watch right here... It is and it isn't a long way from rock and roll. Here are some of the things which as a songwriter make me jealous of the poet: a vocabulary that includes 'half-assed', 'catechism', 'insurance company' and 'tea bag' (it would take me the next ten years to get 'tea bag' into a song). There's his humour: his description of Marilyn Monroe as shining 'like a freshly polished Granny Smith apple/Before avid human fangs bite into it' ('A Special Meeting'). I love 'God As An Unmarried Mother'. In one poem he has Brendan Behan at the Last Supper, in another the holy meal is interrupted by a bomb scare. Then again...

God is a Bomb.
To get the best results, handle carefully,
Time properly, choose a fruitful place
Where you can turn murder into martyrdom...
('Before My Time')

I prefer:

There's only one way to treat God:
Walk up to Him and kiss Him.
He appreciates the direct approach.
Mess around, you'll miss Him.
('Before My Time')

I love this book. I had it with me for twenty chaotic, dizzy days, in Dublin, Paris and Morocco making a video. There, with more than just excess baggage and a most unholy family, the words of this Irish poet made strange sense, words like eyes finding us out as we got lost in the dark, dank streets of Fez. Its dark passageways, its cackles of laughter, its call to prayer, its opium faces all conspired to make the labyrinthine journey of this book visible. Its mad juxtaposition of past/present, Ireland/Middle East plausible even. In more than just my own mind there will always be a smell of this tome of a book. I hope I am not getting off the point, there is light here, bright white light, but if you do find Jesus, you know Judas is just round the corner and he knows... it's got to be-e-e perfect!

GAY BYRNE

Brendan Kennelly on the *Late Late Show*

I am sitting looking out on a spring blossomed rowan tree backed in the distance by a hawthorn hedge, subtly enchanted by the evening sun and slightly bothered by an unexpected breeze. It is quieting and relaxing and ever so satisfying. I am filled with gladness. I find myself smiling, laughing inside as I recall a time when Brendan Kennelly complimented my reading of a poem from *Moloney Up and At It* on the *Late Late Show*. He had been exhorting us to give reason its place and to open our hearts. He asserted that 'there is no receptacle as open as your heart. It's in everybody. There is nothing unusual about it.' He told me that I had lived, for a moment, in his poem. 'Similarly,' he insisted, 'you can let anything live in you if you choose to do so...you can also choose to lock it out.' I was very moved by Brendan's line of thought on that occasion. And now he is back in my head, he has me laughing at myself and thinking how often, on the merry-go-round of work and commitments, I forget his reminder and allow myself to lock out and take for granted such simple, yet ongoing, life-enhancing images and experiences with which life continues to do me the honour.

On the same evening Brendan was talking about freedom and was of the opinion that the imagination, art, music and conversation were freedom-inducing. He told us, 'When I hear Dubliners talking I sense freedom. They are the best talkers in the world.' When I queried whether they were better talkers than the Kerry people, he replied: 'Far better, far better. But Kerrymen are more eloquent. They are wiser but they will not admit it. Dubliners are witty people, they will talk particularly about things they don't know about with the utmost authority. It is a kind of popular infallibility.'

Conversation about freedom and the imagination led us onto fact and fantasy, themes on which Brendan held very definite views. 'The fact that you rebel against fact doesn't mean that you embrace fantasy,' he said and elaborated quite simply, 'if you allow your life to be dominated by electricity bills, revenue commissioners and various other forms of tyranny, you'd never be free at all.' That is when he thought of that lovely thing that Patrick Kavanagh said: 'If you happen to see me walking along Baggot Street and giving the odd jump as I walk along the street, do not be perturbed, I'm simply having a visit from the Holy Ghost.' All of this had meandered out of a discussion on *Moloney Up and At It* which contain poems based on true stories and which Brendan told us are about 'the enjoyment of outrageous moments. We are coming to a point in Irish life where we need to recover outrageous moments.' That was back in 1983 and, indeed, we have recovered many outrageous moments since.

Anyway, 'Moloney' had told Brendan that 'you've got to understand that life is joyful and irrational and that facts are for those who love power'. And we had to put that in our pipes and smoke it.

Love him or loathe him, Brendan is alert; his thoughts flitter hither and thither, and he is brave because he not only allows his thoughts to intermingle and come together but he is prepared to publicly share this process as it happens. In this he challenges his listeners not only to think and reflect but also to enjoy the process.

It is difficult, almost embarrassing, to put pen to paper about a writer as eloquent and imaginative and generous with his thoughts and feelings as is Brendan Kennelly. Over the years he has spoken to me about many subjects on the *Late Late Show* (Cromwell, Ireland, Irish Characters, Christianity, Alcoholism, Life, Love, Education, Academia). On every occasion he has managed to be charming and thought-provoking. Whether reading his work or talking with him on or off the airwaves, I can honestly say that he has never failed to leave a notion or a thought lingering, irking, provoking, challenging, haunting, badgering, amusing or bemusing some aspect of my mind or being. No, he is not larger than life. The thing about Brendan is that he is real, he is earthy, he is thinking, he is exploring, he is creating. He has a thought and a feeling on all aspects of his living. Always, there is an intensity, a sincerity more often than not softened by his teasing eyes and his charming smile. He is a playful person. In playing with his own thoughts and feelings, he plays with yours, too.

Perhaps, rather than talking about him, it would be more appropriate to attempt to recollect a little more of the experience which permits me to talk about him so.

One of my first encounters with Brendan is memorable because he was telling me, privately, about a recurring dream which featured his, then deceased, parents, who, he said, came back to him to talk about things. His sincerity at that time intrigued me and, later, on the *Late Late Show*, I asked him about such dreams. He said, 'if you limit your experience just to now, then you're really not getting the full flavour out of your life. That is why you should admit the dream. Let it in. Let people into you who have vanished from you because I don't believe that people are dead. I happen to believe that there is life there but we exclude it. This makes us poor. If we could admit the dead into our lives, we'd be richer people.' Agree or disagree, one had to think about it.

Another time, he was talking about poetry and people's inhibitions, when, out of the blue, he made us all laugh when he announced that 'respectability is a daylight disease'. His cheek is always infectious and when we stopped laughing, he went on to explain that

> after midnight somehow or another a new freedom creeps into the soul. To me that's the area where poetry enquires into. You have to look at that moment where they shed all these inhibitions. They shed the whole disease of respectability and they become suddenly free. They tell you what happened to them. They tell you in a language that is uninhibited. That's the kind of thing that I think poetry is about. I don't think it should bother with this recording of neurosis. I really can understand why modern poetry has really failed to attract people because who wants to hear about your neurosis? Who wants to hear about your inhibitions? What we want to hear about is songs of genuine freedom – how you feel when you are free.

Christianity is another subject about which I recall vivid contributions from Brendan. He told us that he had hoped that writing his epic poem all about Cromwell would expunge and clear out certain kinds of feelings about Christianity. As it turned out, the experience deepened his need to understand aspects of Christianity. 'What I'd really like to do for the rest of my life,' he told us, 'is to write a poem about Christianity, to try to understand what it is, to try to understand the connection between Christianity and violence, the connection between ideas of Christ and murder. What it is that makes people reared in the Christian tradition walk in and kill each other.' And so, he told us, he turned from the topic to the bawdy *Moloney* which is about 'the comic side of Christianity, about the resurrection, about the side of Christianity which is not emphasised, about the subject of joy'.

On the subject of Christianity, I remember his line that 'we are a better race of Pagans than we are of Christians' and his insistence that 'if we were human enough we would be divine – if people weren't afraid and didn't impose themselves on others; if they could accept their humanity and redevelop their capacity for love and attention and contact and whatever, if you could do that you couldn't seperate your divinity from your humanity.'

With regard to Christian missionary work, Brendan respected the missionary's desire to help the poor and acknowledged that there was nothing more noble. However, he took issue with what he called 'spiritual imperialism' and said that 'distinction has to be drawn between that activity (helping the poor) and the activity to spiritually convert somebody to a way of looking at life which is not natural or culturally inevitable for that person involved'. Of course, this line of thinking did not hold water with many Irish viewers and provoked an audience member into calling him a 'big baby'. To which Brendan replied: 'You are a fairly typical Irish woman because you see all men as babies.' Whatever one's view of Brendan that evening, we were teased into exploring our own views about a subject most central to Irish life, Irish thinking and Irish behaviour.

On another occasion, we were discussing what makes men attractive to women and women attractive to men. Brendan gave a lighthearted start to the discussion when I asked him what kind of a woman he'd be attracted to and he replied, 'I like a woman who'd put up with me.' Company-keeping was a phrase used for dating when Brendan was growing up and for Brendan company-keeping 'was making abnormal what was the most normal thing in the world'. When I pressed him to elaborate on his ideal woman he said that women complete a man's nature somewhat and that every man has an ideal woman in his mind. Pressed further, he told us: 'I like dark hair, I like white skin. I like laughing eyes, I like playful lips, I like shoulders that are kind of waddling or dancing and I like comicality. I like people that are laughing at you and that you never know whether they are laughing at you, with you or because of you and kind of sending you up. I like playfulness above all.' So, I asked him what turned him off women and he replied, 'indulgence in sustained sourness'.

His views on sex were no less definite. He recalled someone who said that 'sex is the greatest fun you can have without laughing'. He insisted that 'sex is not just what is climactic or what happens in bed. The restriction of sexuality to simple expressions of physical sexuality is a gross distortion of it. I think to worry about manifestations of it, expression of it only in bed is to limit people's enjoyment of each other. An awful lot of people who don't make love in bed enjoy each other for their talk, for their crack. Bantering,' he said, 'is a beautiful form of sexuality.'

Brendan has a great respect for love and announced that 'there should be a National Love Day. Since we concentrate our minds in other ways to honour saints and the bank holidays and everything,' he argued, 'why can we not honour the most primal urge in all of us?' I asked him how we could do this and he replied simply, 'by making love everywhere all day long'.

He went on to talk about senses and emphasised that 'the senses are the gateways of knowledge... I think that a sharpening of those senses, that to me is a sexual activity, an educational activity, a spiritual activity. I don't like categorising. I think we have done too much of it, of that kind of categorising in Ireland. It is time we saw that this sexual activity is a normal part of so many other activities and should be freely indulged in.'

Brendan always had a word or two on reason and rationality. I recall him saying, 'a reasonable man who is afraid of his own madness is paradoxically to me, a mad man. A person who doesn't allow his nature enough to let himself go fully in a certain situation – that man is a bit mad. The person, then, who doesn't allow reason to come into his life is lost. A complete personality should have the two elements balanced in him.'

Brendan's acceptance of both reason and madness makes him an excellent teacher. I remember him talking about education and insisting that praise stimulates. 'Praise youth and it will flourish,' he said. A thinker himself, he advocates thinking in education. He said that we cannot isolate education and simply consider it alone. 'There are a lot of "haves" and "have nots" in Ireland today. It's the deepest partition that there is in the country. My simple desire and ambition is to take fear out of teaching. Instead of making people walk into a room at the end of a year and sit down and do four questions on Shakespeare in two hours – why not tell the people the questions beforehand and let them think about them and cut out the fear, cut out the neurosis, cut out the despair and depression and even the suicidal tendencies in students.' In his insistence that we encourage individuality, Brendan does not part with the usefulness of memory. I recall his rueful reflecting that 'memory has gone out of our education system' and insisting that 'it is most important to remember poems, to remember slices, pieces of literature. People often remember things for 50 to 60 years and they come to them at moments when they need a little consolation. It is very amazing how much a poem can bring you a bit of comfort if you say it or a piece out of the Bible. Memory is not in favour anymore and I think it's a pity.' I found myself agreeing with him and I'm sure he prompted many teachers and parents to consider whither the education of our young people.

Another subject on which Brendan gave food for thought was on drink and the dark side of drink – alcoholism. He entertained us about 'blackouts' when you absolutely 'weren't there but at the same time you were there with such intensity that the people around you couldn't believe it'. But he moved us most when he talked about the shame and slavery of alcoholism. We laughed when he talked about 'the heroic aura attaching to the great drinkers – a fellow who could drink 30 to 40 pints on a Sunday, after a match, was a great man'. But we were sobered when he explained, 'that's a public reflection of the self-deception of an alcoholic' and when he elaborated on the slavery attached to such self-deception: 'Whoever said slavery was done away with I think was wrong. Alcoholism is a form of slavery. It's a perverted love affair with a bottle – you fall in love with a bottle and you will do anything to stay with that lady...you devote your life...you arrange your life. Alcoholics can be very clever – often very intelligent, they devote their entire intelligence to arranging their life so that they'll satisfy their own needs and crush, sometimes, the needs of others.' He told us that it was very hard to admit to being a slave and said, 'you actually feel free. The thing about alcoholism is that it provides you with a world of illusion in which you can range from heroism, to gallantry, to being the big man, to being whatever you like. In that world, you'll find support. Dublin is architecturally designed to facilitate the alcoholic – you'll meet people who will cooperate in your world of illusion.' On being freed from the slavery of alcoholism and living life without alcohol, he told us: 'Alcoholism is an extraordinary egotism. You become self-obsessed, everything is related to yourself. When you stop it you get your memory back – getting time back and appreciating other people is one of the great gifts of being freed from that slavery.'

Bless him, Brendan does use his regained time to its fullest and he does appreciate the people and the circumstances around him in his actions and in his writings. It cannot have been easy for him to tell us how his friend, Terence Brown, during his drinking days told him, 'you're very boring...you are a bore...That kind of hurt me.' I have often felt that because Brendan was so open, so generous with his feelings, that he was vulnerable and that he exposed himself to hurt when he spoke on the *Late Late Show*. I am sure that, sometimes, he was hurt. I commend his bravery in sharing himself and his experience and his views so publicly.

Like all of us, I know that Brendan is responsible for breaking many hearts, causing much grief to himself more than to others. I also know that he has challenged and continues to challenge his dark side. He continues to worry and wonder about this life we live. Most importantly, I know that he has been the source of much physical and spiritual comfort to our viewers and to countless numbers of people with whom he has come into contact on his travels, in his moochings around the city, in his teaching and in his writings. I know several writers who owe him for the lift he gave out of confusion and, sometimes, despair. He has given us much food for thought. Most of all he has provided the sustenance of laughter. I think that I would be right in saying that his view would be that he was always as privileged as the person who felt privileged to have encountered him.

Many of my references to Brendan Kennelly may not be entirely accurate and many are, I acknowledge, taken out of context. I hope that the literary Brendan will forgive such liberty. Back to where I started, Brendan's thoughts on the senses come back to me and I realise that I do not know or cannot recall the colour of his eyes of this man whose face I have pondered and explored on so many occasions when his conversation has mesmerised and engaged me. Point taken Brendan, forgive me. You are indeed a dominant influence on our thinking. Long may you continue and long may you be playful. Thank you for the times.

JOHN G. COONEY

Fortitude

Traditionally, alcohol has always played a major part in Irish life. Over the centuries, our literature, songs and poetry contain many allusions to drink and drinking occasions. Inevitably, this image of conviviality has overshadowed the dangers associated with heavy drinking, leading, in a minority of cases, to alcohol dependency.

Alcoholism or alcohol dependency is now regarded as being due to many causes with social, economic and cultural factors influencing the individual man or woman, vulnerable because of hereditary and/or psychlogical factors, among others, on the road to alcoholism. Because of the ambivalent attitude towards drinking which persists in Ireland, many victims of alcoholism are unaware of the insidious change in their drinking pattern, which indicates a progression into alcohol dependency, until some crisis caused by their abnormal drinking develops in their lives. The fact that the most intelligent of people are often unaware of the deterioration in the different areas of their lives brought about by their drinking demonstrates a necessity for much more public enlightenment on the use and abuse of alcohol, notwithstanding the major advances in recent years in our understanding of the issues involved. As an instance, the basic fact that no alcoholic consciously sets out to develop the condition is often overlooked.

I first met Brendan Kennelly when he came under my care some years ago. I was immediately impressed by his good humour and engaging manner at this difficult time in his life. Very soon I came to realise the regard and esteem in which he was held by a diversity of well-wishers. Hardly a day passed that I was not contacted by friends and family members anxious to do all they could to assist him in his recovery.

Over the following weeks, I came to know Brendan intimately in the course of his treatment and soon appreciated the reasons for his popularity. He is a very warm and sociable man with a great interest in people. Inevitably, in the closed world of a hospital, many of the other people participating in the treatment programme were attracted to him. At all times Brendan was sympathetic and helpful to them.

In line with its philosophy of treating the whole person as well as involving family members and concerned persons, St Patrick's makes considerable use of the Arts to this end. Throughout the hospital, there is on display a large collection of art works, placed there not only for aesthetic reasons but also to allay fears and apprehensions experienced by so many people when confronted by psychiatric illness. Poetry readings are encouraged, and Brendan responded readily to an invitation to participate in these sessions. His contributions in St Patrick's and its associated hospital, St Edmundsbury, were very well received by both staff and patients.

None of these involvements diverted him from his commitment to the treatment programme. From the earliest days, he was eager to assume the responsibility for his recovery and devoted himself wholeheartedly to this goal.

Following his discharge, Brendan attended an after care group for several years and made a valuable contribution to its activities which are conducted in a manner always serious but never solemn. In this setting, his eloquence in expressing his point of view, his gift of words, and his impish sense of humour became very apparent. On some occasions, his exuberance forced him into an apparently indefensible position when members of the group challenged a particularly outrageous proposition delivered with tongue in cheek. It was fascinating to observe him extricate himself, quite effortlessly, by a flurry of words, like a good boxer pinned in a corner of the ring.

For those who read the work of Brendan Kennelly, it becomes obvious that behind the genial and charming persona is a sensitive and reflective man, subject, like all major poets, to intense feelings and deeply held convictions. He is a sophisticated man with an acute mind and highly observant – qualities which he employed to the full in coming to terms with his alcohol problem and the comprehensive treatment programme to which he was exposed.

Brendan Kennelly is a most generous man, quick to acknowledge his debts to others and anxious at all times to help people in distress. At the individual level, he has made time to comfort and counsel many victims of alcohol in a constructive and discreet fashion. On the national scene, because of his high profile, he has done a great deal to help the cause of alcoholism by his frank account of his own experiences in this area. The notable success he has enjoyed in his distinguished career following his period of treatment has been an inspiration to many victims and their families.

By publicly acknowledging his alcohol problem and coping so admirably with it, Brendan Kennelly has shown a fortitude that is wholly commendable.

KATIE DONOVAN

Brendan Kennelly as Teacher and Anthologist

Recently I bumped into Brendan Kennelly in Bewley's on West-moreland Street, we ate breakfast together and as usual ended up discussing the mysteries of the human psyche. He had just been reading the Bible, or the gospels, or some such religious fare, and had discovered that the two words which Christ uttered with most frequency were 'Fear not'. Since then, even though I am an agnostic, I have been muttering this like a mantra every time life threatens to throw me into a blue funk. And looking at Kennelly's life and works, it seems like an obvious summing up of his philosophy.

As a teacher, he challenged students to confront their fears from day one. 'Somebody quote me the opening line of a novel,' he demanded of my first year English class. We all sat quaking, un-able to remember a thing. He mocked us for a hopeless group of spineless middle-class know-nothings, until a black student on an exchange from Harvard shouted back the opening sentence of *Pride and Prejudice* (which I have remembered ever since then for this very reason): 'It is a truth universally acknowledged, that a single man in possession of a good fortune, must be in want of a wife.'

By our fourth year we were a lot braver and ready to respond to Brendan's adventurous teaching in his 'Mythology in Irish Lit-erature' class. As well as close readings of texts, this included us directing our own productions of Yeats's plays. I remember Alan Gilsenan, who has gone on to direct plays and TV documentaries, directing *Purgatory*. The sole actor, Ger Flanagan, spoke his lines covered with dead leaves which Alan had gathered patiently in a black plastic bag. I remember the flourish with which Alan opened the bag and poured the leaves all over Ger before the play began.

I directed *The Only Jealousy of Emer* (chaotic rehearsals and attempts at choreography beforehand with Maureen Boyle, Pat ffrench and the rest of my cast) and acted in an all-woman version of *At the Hawk's Well* directed by Victoria White, now assistant arts editor of the *Irish Times*. These memories stay bright, in compari-son with countless other classes with other teachers that have long since faded from my mind.

Brendan also asked us to write our own myths in response to some of the sections in *Ulysses*. With the 'Wandering Rocks' seq-uence, for example, we were to write our own stories of wandering through Dublin, and the social rituals involved. I remember Brendan doubling over with laughter as he went through the different forms of greetings you might hear around the city. His favourite was 'How're they hangin?'

He encouraged us to be as outrageous as Joyce. Yet at the same time he assumed calmly that we were reading *Ulysses* alongside Homer's original *Odyssey* every week, and giving both texts a good deal of questioning scrutiny. We did. It was the best way to get to know Joyce's infuriating, irresistible novel.

Those were Brendan's drinking years, and he could give the most lucid and stimulating lectures while claiming he was far from sober. He could also, by reputation, be something of a lad. But the only time I ever saw him put his arm around a student was after she had fainted and fallen off her seat in the middle of one of his lectures. The whole class repaired to Brendan's rooms, where he gave the recovering girl a tot of whiskey, and we went on with the lecture, in amongst the heaps of papers and books with which Brendan invariably surrounds himself.

He was different from our other lecturers in that he was able to quote large chunks of poems by heart, frequently and beautifully. He even did this outside class. It was quite awe-inspiring. Yet at the same time he could tell rude jokes and invite you for a pint in O'Neill's. And behind all of this – even though he was the type to stroll across Front Square and say 'How're ya' to everyone he passed, particularly the porters – there was a core of shyness and reserve. He was, after all, the Prof (as his assistant, Geraldine Mangan, calls him). He was also one of Ireland's foremost poets and spoke casually of rising earlier than any of us considered humanly possible to write his poetry. At that time he was doing a lot of research in connection with *Cromwell*. We couldn't imagine poring over history books unless it was to pass an exam.

Ten years later, remembering all of this, it was with a mixture of excitement and nerves that I responded to Brendan's suggestion that I collaborate with him and A. Norman Jeffares on an anthology by and about Irish women. It was early spring of 1992, in the aftermath of the publication of the first three volumes of *The Field Day Anthology of Irish Writing* which had managed to exclude a lot of Irish women, particularly in the Contemporary Poetry section. I had written a report for the *Irish Times* on the heated debate at the Irish Writers' Centre between some of *The Field Day Anthology* section editors and a large number of irate women and men.

Brendan believed that an anthology about Irish women, by Irish writers of either sex and in many different genres, would be a good antidote to the bad feelings created by the Field Day debacle. It would be wide-ranging, thematically based – a book people would read. It would feature writing by women and writing by men, and it would not stop at putting in articulations of prejudice, ignorance or bigotry. It would be lively, colourful, passionate, controversial.

As Irish people know from his voice-overs on advertisements for cars and butter, Brendan can sell anything. In this case, he was preaching to a converted audience: my mind was bursting with ideas. I was dying to get my teeth into the project. I just hoped that A. Norman Jeffares would also be enthusiastic about having me on the editorial team.

Some months later we all met, A. Norman Jeffares (or Derry as I quickly began to know him) having flown over especially from Scotland, where he currently lives. We each had sheaves of photocopies. I even had bags of books, because I hadn't had time to get photocopies of everything I wanted to show them.

We spent two days of discussing, laughing, arguing, shuffling around in heaps of paper on the floor, taking notes, reading out our favourite extracts to each other, all talking at once, scratching our heads, making lists, making tea and forgetting to drink it. Considering I was the junior, I ended up bossing them both around. I kept butting in with my ideas. I forgave myself because, after all, I was the only woman on the team, and women were at the centre of the anthology. Luckily, they seemed to feel the same. When there was a disagreement, Brendan almost automatically took my side, and Derry was very accommodating.

There was a nice symmetry in the fact that Derry had once been Brendan's teacher (at Leeds University) just as Brendan had once been mine. Now I could contribute a little to their learning process, introducing them to contemporary women writers such as Moya Roddy and Angela Greene.

As time wore on, however, our so-called fields of expertise melted in a free-for-all where we raved about anyone we thought was good, regardless of era or genre. Behind it all was Brendan, always asking questions, usually 'Why not?' He was a natural at brainstorming. Ideas flowed from him like lava. Sometimes Derry and I would grow exhausted just by listening to him. We'd have to ask him to stop. Most of his ideas were good; many were brilliant. It was his keen shaping intelligence that structured the book into twelve thematic sections. While Derry and I were rather woolly and safe at this sort of work, Brendan would dream up topics with names such as 'Shapechangers' (for a section on woman as symbol and supernatural being) and 'The Bit of Strange' (a Dublin expression for an affair, which was a perfect heading for a section on women's illicit loves).

Sometimes Derry and I would begin a small plan, like a wavery house of cards, and Brendan would come rushing in and change everything. Usually it would be an improvement. If we didn't like it, he'd be only too ready to admit that perhaps he'd been mistaken. But his restless, questioning, inspirational approach ensured that we never got complacent. Nothing was sacred; and yet everything was. This we had to remember. The extract he chose about the anonymous drug addict Lisa was as important as anything by Maria Edgeworth or Lady Gregory.

When it came to the more mundane business of keeping extracts short, tracking down elusive texts, and making photocopies, however, he showed another talent: that of delegating. Derry and I found ourselves looking after almost all of this side of the anthology.

In the meantime, Brendan had already put together an anthology of his own favourite poems entitled *Between Innocence and Peace: Favourite Poems of Ireland* into which he had poured the same daring mix of ingredients. He is still grieved by the fact that reviewers of the book remained impervious to the shaping intelligence that went into determining the sequence of the poems. As with the ingredients of *Ireland's Women*, each was intended to start a dialogue with the one beside it (reviewers were a little more clued in to this design in *Ireland's Women* simply because we spelt out our strategy in our introductions to the book).

And willy-nilly, before *Ireland's Women* was even properly put to bed, Brendan proposed yet another anthology, this time one of writings about Dublin. *Dublines* had been brewing in his brain for some time. He asked me to help him put it together.

As with *Ireland's Women*, our first task was to divide the book into sections and decide what themes would govern each section. He showed the same talent for inventive approaches and titles; the same inimitable skill for delegation. We had intense talks in Bewley's and in various rooms at Trinity, sorting through piles of material. This time we could only have six sections and 300 pages instead of the twelve sections and over 500 pages which we were allowed for *Ireland's Women*. I wrung my hands over the small number of pages we were allotted, but Brendan kept me laughing, envisaging what the real Dubs would say when they read an anthology put together by a cute Kerry hoor and a Wexford yellowbelly. Every hurdle I discovered seemed to dwindle into insignificance as we swept through the work. Brendan wanted to confront all the myths of Dublin: those of the outsiders as well as the insiders, and this involved looking behind the cosy chatty boozy little city to the grim incestuous character-assassination that is part of Dublin's nature too. He knew how affronted people would be by the latter and he relished their anticipated annoyance.

One thing that has always impressed me about Brendan is his lack of fear when it comes to looking at the dark side of the human psyche, including his own; on the contrary, it fascinates him with its seductive mystery, pain and absurdity. He is well aware how much this can upset the equilibrium of other people, but as far as he is concerned, there's nothing like offering them a challenge.

I remember him speaking about the foolhardy nature of the hero in his lectures on Yeats's plays about Cúchulain. Brendan's fearlessness can at times seem foolhardy, as though inviting a hostile response (and he gets plenty of these, in amongst the clusterings of fans). The challenge he offers can seem too much to some people. But for a man and poet of his generation, he is virtually alone in his determination to continue to question smugness or complacency in himself and in the world around him, to embody that immortal phrase 'Fear Not' and to bear it like an inspirational torch into everything he does and into the lives of others.

Long may the torch burn, Kennelly.

HARRY FERGUSON

'Iron Brendan': Brendan Kennelly and Images of Masculinity, Wounding and Healing

Although I worked in the same institution as Brendan for five years, I know him less in terms of direct contact while at Trinity than through the media and his public appearances. In the few direct contacts I had with him, I have to say I found him lyrical, ebullient and unpredictable.

Thus, how I "know" Kennelly is as a product of the global village; as virtual reality! It corresponds to how the effect of advanced modern communication is such that one can be more connected to someone to whom one is talking on the telephone at the other side of the world than with a person who is in the same room; or in the case of Brendan and myself, more connected to someone through seeing them on TV than when co-existing, separated by one floor of the Arts Building in TCD – my ceiling was Brendan's floor. 'More and more, media make us "direct" audiences to performances that happen in other places and give us access to audiences that are not "physically present",' writes the sociologist Joshua Meyrowitz.[1] The traditional connection between 'physical setting' and 'social situation' becomes undermined with the result that mediated social situations construct new communalities and differences between preconstituted forms of social experience.[2] 'We could say,' observes Urlick Beck, that 'people meet every evening around the world at *the village green* of television and consume the news.'[3]

As a sociologist, as opposed to a literary theorist (however much the disciplinary boundaries are weakening these days), I cannot claim to know a great deal about Brendan Kennelly's artistic canon. I find the method and process of how we know Kennelly to be as significant as what we know. There is something in itself interesting and instructive about this form of knowing and I intend here to discuss Kennelly in terms of, and through, images and representation. I am particularly interested in Kennelly *the man*. I use the term "man" here quite literally, in terms of him as a gendered individual, rather than some undifferentiated representative of "mankind". Three particular images of Kennelly come to mind – all of them of him on television – that I shall call the *masculine*; the *wounded*; and the *healer*.

On a *Late Late Show* in the mid-1980s, discussing the subject of the Irish and the drink, Gay Byrne pressed Brendan to account for the meaning of drink in Irish life. 'The Irishman gets more pleasure out of the pint he gets after closing time than any amount of them before it,' Brendan averred. This was said with that structure of feeling that animates all Brendan's observations. One could feel oneself in the pub with him, part of a global community of (after-hours) pint drinkers, him slapping his fist on the bar, roaring 'more pints please...' It brings to mind Eamon Morrisey's opening to his brilliant one-man show *Just the One*: 'In the beginning there was darkness... And then a voice said, "go round the back and ye'll get in!"'

Kennelly's celebration of after hours drinking and the Irish culture of the pint is a vote of confidence in the subversion, psychic anarchy and resistance to rules that mark the Irish character... and whatever you're having yourself. It is also a gracious slap on the back for men. For me, Kennelly's world is fundamentally a male world, and is exemplified by the culture of the pub which is a masculine culture. Kennelly is a survivor of the male culture of the pub and the pint, which through his own self-confessed addiction, has sorely wounded him. Yet he continues to celebrate and even to glorify that culture.

This takes on added piquancy in the light of the second image of Brendan, also from a *Late Late Show* in the early 1990s, and also on the subject of alcohol. Brendan spoke with typical passion about his own addiction and recovery from alcoholism. This included reading the poem, 'The Healer', which he dedicated to his psychiatrist, John Cooney, who was present beside Gay on the panel:

> The horror of accusing morning light
> Condemns me to another hideous day.
> Did someone cry? What did I do last night?
> Was someone hurt? Insulted? What did I say?
> My hands are crazy, blood streaks my eyes,
> Jeering images flash havoc through my mind,
> My mouth is full of muck and stupid lies,
> I'm hell, I know hell's taste and smell and sound.
>
> Healer, I hear you speak: your head and heart
> Help many a suffering man and woman
> While I, like countless women and men,
> Am learning how to tend and heal each hurt
> With candid, gentle words, profoundly human.
> Thanks to you, hope lives again.[4]

Some of this may be hard to swallow. In following such an abstinence model of surviving an addiction to alcohol, Brendan seems to have replaced downing pints with swallowing the medical model and disease concept of alcoholism. Other approaches to alcohol addiction which emphasise various social factors and the utility of controlled drinking appear to be ignored in the healing model that Brendan Kennelly celebrates. I suppose if it works for him, then who am I to judge? What is striking is the dependence underlying his deference to the healing power of the psychiatric expert, and his willingness to acknowledge and honour that debt.

This observation can be deepened further through the third image which comes from an RTE *Live At Three* programme in 1994 which I came upon quite by chance. Brendan was judging a poetry competition and told the story of going to Waterford to judge a Heat. There he listened to a woman who stood up and read her poem which told of her experience of being a survivor of child sexual abuse. For Kennelly, the honesty and courage of such a public disclosure expressed through art reflected how 'We're beginning to come to terms with the darker side of ourselves as a society; we're starting to grow up.'

He's at least partially right. Disclosure of previously hidden problems like child sexual abuse has indeed increased dramatically in recent years. This is Kennelly the healer; the healer Kennelly. More specifically, Kennelly creating spaces that can help wounded people to heal; enable us as a society to face the ghosts of the past. I am far from convinced that men like Kennelly should be encouraged to open up these spaces for women survivors. Yet, his words on the television undoubtedly will have encouraged others to find healing through art and in disclosure of the hidden pain that constitutes childhood sexual abuse.

Above all, perhaps, what Brendan understands best is the corrosive impact of silence and secrets, on an individual; a community; a culture. 'If people who have secrets all over came out,' he told Gay Byrne, 'we'd all be so much richer for it. The increased happiness of one person contributes to the happiness of all Irish people.' In his poem 'My Dark Fathers' he articulates the cultural impact of the silence around the Famine and the legacy of unresolved grief, shame and loss:

> I celebrate the darkness and the shame
> That could compel a man to turn his face
> Against the wall, withdrawn from light so strong
> And undeceiving, spancelled in a place
> Of unapplauding hands and broken song.

In acknowledging his own woundedness (his addiction etc) Brendan opens up spaces for others to tell their secrets. 'The prostitute, the drunk, the leper, is in all of us; in me,' he told the *Late Late Show*. But while he clearly appreciates the sacredness of confessing, I fear that Brendan does not know when to stop; how it has to be made safe to tell and the kind of boundaries that need to be placed around disclosure and supports put in place for the aftermath of the secret being out. For me, this relates to his position as a man. The unifying theme in these three images of Brendan is masculinity, pain and violence. Kennelly the man spells both opportunity and danger; wounding and healing.

In embodying these images of the masculine, wounding and healing, Brendan's work (inadvertently) touches on some similar themes to those being addressed by the, so called, men's movement and the new academic sub-discipline of the critical study of men and masculinities. Especially relevant here is the perspective that is known as the mytho-poetic men's movement and popularised by the American poet and writer on men, Robert Bly, in his international bestseller, *Iron John*. Central to Bly's work is a concern to use art forms such as poetry, myths and story-telling to enable men to (re)discover a role in the advanced modern world; to get (back) in touch with their masculine self, the Iron John within. The focus here is on the loss of collective certainty and ritual that modernity has brought about for men and which arises from the loss of initiatory experiences and transitions into adult manhood. And poetry is one way for men to (re)connect with their inner lives, the imagination. As the three leading exponents of the mytho-peotic men's movement argue: 'Men blame their own lives for a deficiency in the culture. For without the fanciful delicacy and the powerful truths that poems convey, emotions and imagination flatten out.' [5]

It is no coincidence then that Kennelly is the only artist whose work is featured twice in a ground-breaking new book on Irish fathers and sons, *Fathers and Sons*, which takes its inspiration from the mytho-poetic men's movement.[6] Nor is it a coincidence, then, that I should link Kennelly with Bly, whose work has frequently been labelled as anti-feminist, with its implicit appeal to an essential form of the 'masculine' and authentic kind of 'man' within, that must be rediscovered. As feminists argue, it is this 'Iron Man' within, and without, who is a product of patriarchy and the *cause* of so many of our problems. Any straightforward appeal to a recapturing of him cannot therefore be seen as any possible solution to the wounds perpetrated by men. Thus, any uncritical celebration of men and masculinity in this vein is dangerous. But while the politics and aesthetics of the mytho-poetic men's movement have been seriously questioned, what has been grossly mis-understood is that what is offered here is a methodology: a means to working with men and accessing their experience which can promote genuine personal and political change, and promote the well-being of women, children and men. That sense in which 'working in poetry and myth with men is a therapy for the culture at its psychic roots'.[7]

It is not so much that Kennelly's work consciously seeks to cel-ebrate an essentialist view of man as such – the Iron Brendan within us all. It is rather that, whether he likes it not, he *embodies* just such a (wounded) masculine character and his poetry is just such a form of therapy for our culture at its psychic roots. The silences that Kennelly draws attention to from the Famine have a generic relevance to our culture, men, women and children alike. But it is among and between men that the most pervasive gaps and silences persist in Irish society, which are at the core of sus-taining men's power and their (hidden) pain.[8] It is the secrets of men that Brendan really shatters. He is a man's poet; a piss-artist for all Irish men.

I would be surprised indeed were Brendan aware of the contra-dictions that he embodies in terms of the dialectics of the mascu-line, wounding and healing. While I have read him on women, including his anthology on writings about Irish women, *Ireland's Women* (with Katie Donovan and A. Norman Jeffares), he gives little sense of being reflective on his masculinity. He seems a very unself-conscious man as a man; the quintessential "liver out" of masculinity, rather than questioning it. Why should he? it could be protested. My answer is because while it can benefit men, it can also endanger women. It is this unreconstructed sense of him as a (wild) man – Iron Brendan – which accounts in large measure for the sense of danger that surrounds Brendan; of boundary-less-ness. That sense of rage is never too far from the surface; a mas-culine pain. Violence. Something nasty is always at risk of pouring out. This "leakage" of wounds and wounding is ever present in his most recent collection, *Poetry My Arse* (1995), in which the themes of violence and hatred are all-pervasive. This is also good. For there is nothing unusual in this in Brendan the man. His uniqueness is in his courage and very public demonstrations of his dependence and vulnerability as a man.

And yet the discomfort is also at times too much to bear. Per-haps it is this sense of danger and boundary-lessness which accounts for the fact that I did not find this an easy piece to write and the fact that, if I am brutally honest, I don't trust him. I have been struggling to find a nice, defensible way of saying that. But now that I have travelled a sort of journey with Brendan and made the effort to get closer to him, I don't need to say it. I don't feel it. I still have real reservations about the images of masculinity that he represents, although I now have to concede enormous respect for the spaces of healing that he opens up, despite himself. I have grown to love him more as a man. This is all part of what men like Kennelly must carry: the projections and discomforts of men; of our fathers, the drink, the pain, the shite, the glory: the masculine. He puts himself out there, and he has to carry what we place on him. In the context of the global village, this relationship is really about us, ourselves, and not about Kennelly at all. In helping us to acknowledge our secrets, break through silence, Kennelly, despite and because of himself, heals by acting as a focus for the love and hate that is our projections...He is all our Dark Fathers.

REFERENCES

1: Joshua Meyrowitz: *No Sense of Place* (Oxford: Oxford University Press, 1985).

2: Anthony Giddens: *Modernity and Self-Identity: Self and Society in the Late Modern Age* (Cambridge: Polity, 1991, p.84).

3: Urlick Beck: *Risk Society* (1992, p.133, original emphasis).

4: Brendan Kennelly: 'The Healer'. Published in John. G. Cooney, *Under the Weather: Alcohol Abuse and Alcoholism: How to Cope* (Dublin: Gill and Macmillan, 1991).

5: Robert Bly, James Hillman and Michael Meade (eds): *The Rag and Bone Shop of the Heart: Poems for Men* (New York: HarperCollins, 1992).

6: Tom Hyde (ed.): *Fathers and Sons* (Dublin: Wolfhound Press, 1995). The poems are 'I See You Dancing, Father' and 'My Dark Fathers'.

7: Robert Bly et al: *The Rag and Bone Shop of the Heart.*

8: Hugh Arthurs, Harry Ferguson and Edmond Grace: 'Celibacy, Secrecy and the Lives of Men', *Doctrine and Life*, 45 (September 1995), pp.459-68.

ALLEN FIGGIS

Good Soul Surviving

By 1960 the old book-selling firm of Hodges Figgis was expanding rapidly in a number of areas. Buoyed by some success of a first major publishing adventure with MacLysaght's *Irish Families* (1957) I thought (rightly) that it would be a pleasurable achievement if we could plough something back into the system by encouraging Irish writers while insulating the main firm from the risks attached. Hence the formation of my own minuscule publishing company, with plenty of enthusiasm and altruism, but very small capital. Perhaps there was an element of vanity, perhaps an outlandish gamble on that elusive best-seller, but there was a genuine hope of creating a new opening for young writers. There were several experimental "first novels" by authors who invariably promised to write something saleable next time, and I have always felt that we made at least one small contribution to the corpus of Irish literature by the publication of *The Week-end of Dermot and Grace*, by Eugene Watters. I believe that this remarkable work will eventually come to be recognised as something of considerable literary importance.

Obviously, when Brendan Kennelly came on the scene his work was ideally suited to the programme, because of what I believed to be the exceptional quality of his poetry. I cannot say that the earth actually moved when we first met, but I do know that there was an instant rapport between us. It was not just the entirely loveable Kerry charm and the infectious laughter. Beneath the boyish badinage of thirty years ago I sensed at once a serious person with a great depth of humanity. It is hard for me to think of the young Kennelly without recalling my mother, with whom there was also an immediate bond of warm friendship. Frances, my co-director, belonged to a sterner generation of people who behaved properly and this gave her a somewhat proprietorial attitude towards the young. Five minutes after my introduction to her of the budding genius she prodded the poetical paunch and made a well-remembered exit with the admonition, 'Brendan, you are drinking too much. You need to lose weight.' This was precisely what his own mother had been telling him and he was delighted to have the diagnosis confirmed by an expert. Frances and he became firm allies and he visited her regularly, accepting meals and maternal dicta in return for poems read, or spoken from memory. There is a nice collection of first editions with affectionate dedications to her.

I had already, in 1963, published Brendan's first novel, *The Crooked Cross*, when by 1966 'the gift' was discovered. '*Getting up Early* promises well,' indeed. It was soon followed by collections such as *Good Souls to Survive, Dream of a Black Fox* and *Love Cry*, the style and clarity of which established him as a leading Irish poet. All the time the depth of sensitivity was never quite camouflaged by the earthy jocularity and I came to admire the great integrity in Brendan's writing. Each poem was honed down until every word was essential, fitting precisely the colour and pattern of the fabric.

Once, when I suggested the opening line 'He mounted her' was too farmyard an image for such a delicate poem of human relations as 'Love Cry', he explained that it could not be altered as this was the phrase which had been given to him. He seemed to speak of an entity outside of himself. Padraic Colum conveyed the same idea. We would meet for dinner either here or in New York and the young old man would always enjoy the evening as my guest. Before we parted, however, he would make his contribution with, 'Now, I'll give you a poem.' It was as if he were passing on a precious possession.

One day Brendan breezed into my office with a tall willowy blonde American girl and took me completely by surprise when he announced that she intended to marry him. No doubt hoping to cover my shock he reduced the situation to the level of 'country matters'. As I had barely finished shaking hands with the stranger, the familiarity left Peggy and me suspended in an awkward silence, which was never fully broken.

An episode in *The Florentines* (1967), described in fiction but based on fact, came to mind. The narrator (Brendan) is sitting at his window and observes a young girl stepping out from behind one vehicle into the path of another. He can see the inevitability of disaster but is quite impotent to do anything about it. As usual it was Frances who focused on the essential. Consigning a lifetime of moral scruple to the refuse bin she declared that 'Brendan should never marry anyone. It will ruin his muse. Let him take a mistress if he really needs "that sort of thing".'

After this he and I met only infrequently over a number of years. Following a fashionable coronary I retired from the business, which was sold, and adopted a somewhat monastic lifestyle as administrator of Christ Church Cathedral in Dublin.

Fulfilling for a time my mother's early prognosis, Brendan became seriously ill. I used to see him regularly from my office window marching towards the hospital with the resolution of a guardsman on parade. There was a look on his face compounded of utter misery and clear determination to go through with the cure at whatever cost. At this time some tentative suggestions of a meeting were shrugged off and I sensed that there was something which must be achieved without outside intervention.

He came through all the horror intact and strengthened, but the scars are perhaps evident in the prolonged and trenchant attack on the many-faceted hypocrisies in our society. *The Book of Judas* cuts to the roots of the national psyche with surgical precision.

Brendan's ability as a teacher is legendary and I witnessed a quite astonishing example of this when he addressed a large group of Leaving Certificate students from the pulpit of the cathedral. His judgement was impeccable and there was none of the language often used to shock. Instead, he raised the whole occasion to a very high spiritual plane and sent the young audience away fired with a new vision of what poetry is all about. I have seldom seen such rapt attention, or heard more enthusiastic appreciation. He has, I believe, inspired generations of students in this way.

Now he is quite his old jocund self again, albeit with a steely streak well tempered over the years. With meddling curiosity it has occurred to me to wonder if it is perhaps for some quite unselfish reason that the well-known voice recommends a car which he is incapable of driving and a financial institution whose selfless devotion to the well-being of the nation last year built itself a better profit of two hundred and forty million pounds. He is, as he says of himself, a cute hoor in some ways, but the dedication to his poetry is sincere and absolute.

Recently he came to dinner and, as with all good friendships, it was as if we had never parted. He told of a late-night stabbing and robbery which he had experienced. With his quite extraordinary compassion and sense of priority, his concern was not for himself but for the attacker, his needs and society's failure. It is somewhat ironical that I work in a cathedral because I have no taste for ritualistic religiosity, but over the years I have been privileged to meet there scholars of great moral stature. I can think of none with a deeper insight to the mind of the creator than Brendan Kennelly.

His is a trusteeship. The poems are not his, but gospel to be proclaimed: or, as he has put it,

> It came slowly.
> It was a gift that took me unawares
> And I accepted it.
>
> ('The Gift')

36

PADDY FINNEGAN

An Impression of Brendan Kennelly

My acquaintance with this affable Falstaffian guru goes back quite a few years. I heard him wax eloquent and set tables at a roar in late or early sessions in many a hostelry back in the 70s. I marvelled somewhat at the stamina of a man who could fulfil what must be a fairly onerous calling as a university teacher with that of a *bon viveur*, man about town, and yet keep on producing the creative volumes of poetry which have appeared consistently for as long as I can remember.

Of course, in many areas of rural Ireland there was not such a rigid distinction between working for one's living and participating in art or the things of the spirit. Memorable poems and songs have been composed by men and women who would not in their wildest fantasies consider themselves to be creative artists at all. When the artist has acquired self-consciousness as "an artist", he descends into a stygian abyss of convoluted mediocrity and craptic meanderings of consummate absurdity.

Brendan Kennelly does not need to posture, for he is a natural. People who are for real attract other people's interest and respect because the reality and lack of mask can easily be sensed.

In recent months, my own calling in life has dictated that I post myself daily, like a crane at a lake, outside the front gates of Trinity College where I sell the *Big Issues* magazine to passers-by. Readers will be aware, I hope, that this is the famous magazine which helps the homeless and marginalised in our society.

Anyhow, I often have the pleasure of exchanging pleasantries and all sorts of arcane "magpieisms" with this engaging guru of Acadame.

One morning last spring I had occasion to experience him in the role of the Poet-Prophet. I feared that rain was imminent for all the portents, for a deluge seemed to be there, low dark clouds and wind from the Scartaglen direction. Anyhow, I asked the Ballylongford wizard for a meteorological prognostication. He replied in the immortal words: 'There'll be no rain; it'll be as dhry, as dhry as a witch's tit.'

Well, as true as I'm writing this, dear reader, he wasn't gone fifteen minutes when amazingly the cloud dispersed and as our old friend Pythagoras used to say: 'Phoebus played a blinder for the rest of the day.'

The moral of the story surely confirms the belief in the poet as seer.

Voices from Dublin

1

ÅP: 'Excuse me, does the name Brendan Kennelly mean anything to you?'

Woman 1: 'Nothing.'

ÅP: 'You haven't heard anything about him?'

Woman 1: 'Nothing whatsoever, I have no clue who he is, I've never heard of him.'

ÅP: 'OK, thank you very much.'

2

ÅP: 'If I say the name Brendan Kennelly, does that mean anything to you?'

Woman 2: 'Indeed it does.'

ÅP: 'What?'

Woman 2: 'He won the Nobel Peace Prize this year, oh no, he didn't actually, that was Seamus Heaney. Brendan Kennelly, yes, he's a poet.'

ÅP: 'Is that the only thing you know about him?'

Woman 2: 'He's a lovely, cuddly man, a very loveable sort of a character.'

ÅP: 'How do you know about him?'

Woman 2: 'I've read about him in the papers, and…he's been on television quite a lot.'

ÅP: 'Have you read any of his poetry?'

Woman 2: 'I haven't, no, just the odd poem in the paper, but I've never bought any books.'

ÅP: 'OK, thanks.'

3

ÅP: 'Have you heard of Brendan Kennelly?'

Man 1: 'Yes, an Irish poet.'

ÅP: 'Irish poet, yes, is that the only thing you know about him?'

Man 1: 'Yes.'

ÅP: 'Are you familiar with his work?'

Man 1: 'No.'

ÅP: 'How did you know of him?'

Man 1: 'Just that he was the Poet Laureate, or whatever it was, what he got recently.'
ÅP: 'Is that all?'
Man 1: 'That's it.'
ÅP: 'Thank you.'

4

ÅP: 'Does the name Brendan Kennelly ring a bell?'
Man 2: 'Yes, a singer, he's a singer, isn't he?'
ÅP: 'Well…'
Man 2: 'But I don't know more about him.'
ÅP: 'All right, thanks.'

5

ÅP: 'Brendan Kennelly, do you know who he is?'
Woman 3: 'Poet, Nobel Prize in literature, that's all, Trinity lecturer, that's all, really.'
ÅP: 'Is that what you know about him?'
Woman 3: 'I'm afraid so.'
ÅP: 'Thank you.'

6

ÅP: 'Are you familiar with Brendan Kennelly?'
Man 3: 'I know he's a poet.'
ÅP: 'Have you read any of his work?'
Man 3: 'No.'
ÅP: 'Have you heard of him in any other capacity?'
Man 3: 'No. I just know that he has his own special corner in a restaurant nearby. That's where I would have heard of him.'
ÅP: 'Would you recognise him?'
Man 3: 'No.'
ÅP: 'OK, thanks.'

7

ÅP: 'Have you heard of Brendan Kennelly?'
Man 4: 'Not that I can remember, no.'
ÅP: 'You don't recognise the name?'
Man 4: 'No, not really. For a moment I thought it was a singer you were talking about, but it doesn't really ring a bell.'
ÅP: 'No? OK, thanks.'

LIAM GORMAN

The Poet as Management Educator

Brendan Kennelly is a life-long close friend of a life-long close friend of mine. However, our paths only crossed at widely separated intervals at my friend's home. My biding memories of those meetings are of evenings filled with fun and loud laughter, and the stories...particularly the ones of Brendan's life in Dublin's flatland in the 50s. The sheer love of life and joy in living which emanated from Brendan always infected those of us around him, and stayed with us for days afterward.

Coming from a "management" background myself, I felt some trepidation in meeting Brendan. Initially, I feared he might hold some of the stereotypical beliefs which many people in the arts have about those of us who make our living in "commerce" – that we're technocratic, élitist and inhumane in the pursuit of the gods of efficiency and profit. My fears were groundless: over time, I came to the conclusion that if Brendan brought such enrichment to my life, he would have a similar impact on other managers and business people of my acquaintance.

I asked him to come and lecture to a group of managers. As I expected, he did not make himself "precious". He saw an opportunity to meet a group of people out of his normal course, and an opportunity to talk on topics which were not his usual subject matter. His brief was to talk on areas close to managers' hearts: leadership, the nature of work, organisational life.

Knowing Brendan's talent and humour, he could have captivated his audience simply by talking "off-the-cuff". He did not do this. As he talked it became obvious how extensive and considerable his preparation had been. His audience saw this and appreciated his attention to their specific preoccupations. He ranged over history, literature, and biography. More impressively, he shared the fruits of his own experience and illustrated the themes by renditions of his poetry. Throughout, all was leavened by his humour, self-revelation, and self-mockery. He delighted the group by telling of his own short-lived brush with a business career – his senior manager, on learning of Brendan's intention to pursue University studies full-time, informed him that this was a good move for him *and for the company!*

Thereafter, talks by Brendan Kennelly always attracted a full house: a diverse audience of managers from multinational corporations, large and small businesses, semi-state and public servants. Often, managers returned to hear him talk again and again. At question time the discussions always ran seriously over time. Brendan, generous as always, stayed on to have a drink with the groups (although he himself had long since turned his back on the booze). Many hours later he was still talking, listening, questioning, and, of course, sparking off everyone with wit and good humour.

That Brendan Kennelly had a significant impact on those who attended his seminars is beyond doubt. Would it be a cliché or an exaggeration to say he had a "life-changing" effect? Not for some. But I can say with certainty that his talks had a "life-enhancing" impact on all of us present. This I know from observing the behaviour of those attending (up to 120 in number) and from their comments and questions afterward – the majority lingering for many hours to discuss and ruminate upon the themes raised by Brendan.

What exactly did people learn? Principally I believe they learned to question their own outlook and to give their assumptions a good dusting down. They may even have abandoned some of their more cherished, but limiting, intellectual blindfolds. At the conclusion of Brendan's talks the questions did not relate to techniques or procedures or systems but rather they were far more fundamental in nature: What do organisations do to people? Is there a better way? Must work inevitably dehumanise? Can diverse interests within organisations be authentically reconciled or are hostility, defensiveness, low trust and exploitation, inevitable?

Managers live in a demanding, hard, sometimes even brutal environment. Company viability can entail harsh decisions about people, the disposition of resources, and the balancing of interests of various stakeholders in the organisation. The decisions are usually necessary to deflect even worse consequences were they not taken. It is difficult for managers to behave in an altruistic manner towards all. It can be easy for a manager to lose his or her sense of common humanity.

A sense of self-identify and common humanity was awakened in the managers attending Brendan's seminars through hearing his views and his enunciation of his own outlook on life and how he can accept people with different, sometimes repellent, views. I believe this ultimately will modify the blunt edge of the techno-cratic orientation to which life in business makes us prone.

For some time now I have felt that the education of managers would be enhanced by more contact with people from a different background, particularly that of literature and the arts. Observing the effect of Brendan's work with managers has confirmed for me the value of such contact. I wonder, however, is the fruitfulness of Brendan's work too dependent on Brendan? His humour, his attitude and humanity, his unstinting generosity and his unique experiences are just a few of his assets as a teacher. Through these he can build bridges across worlds. If others can do this we will have enriched hugely the educational possibilities for managers.

JACK HANNA

Full Measure

> By what legerdemain
> did such lamentation
> befall the innocent?
> When almost all creatures
> beget their kind,
> whither our benighted tribe?

I still vividly remember the chill down my spine on hearing Brendan Kennelly read those concluding lines from a poem by my son Davoren at the launch of his book of poems, *Not Common Speech*, on a warm April evening in 1990.

It was a convivial evening with friends of Davoren gathered together to celebrate his triumph in publishing his book of poems despite his appalling handicaps (Davoren had no speech and very little physical movement). We had the Voice Squad performing, Ivor Browne gave us a tune on his tin whistle and Máire Ní Bhraonáin of Clannad sang a Donegal song in Irish. Publisher Dermot Bolger spoke and a young friend of Davoren's and I read some of his more accessible and amusing poems – ones that were not included in the book.

Brendan was with us in our celebrations – is he not Ireland's bard of celebration? – but he had been tense and withdrawn earlier in the evening. He was going to give Davoren his full measure.

That is what chilled me to the marrow. Without any sentimentality he described the shocking scale of Davoren's disability but just as forcibly he endorsed the soaring quality of Davoren's poetic spirit.

And then he read – wholeheartedly, powerfully, searingly. Davoren was just 15 at the time. In the face of such rigour and passion in performing his poems, Davoren must have felt like the little boy in his poem 'Famine' – 'astounded to be there'.

Our first contact with Brendan occurred when Davoren's mother, Brighid, was still liaising with the School of Education in Trinity College as she struggled to finish her M.Ed. thesis. She was intrigued by the legend of Brendan and his love for women, so there was a certain "divilment" in her approaching him, but a sure instinct guided her to one of the great artistic encouragers of twentieth-century Ireland.

She met the legend but she also met the pragmatic, astute and trustworthy ally. She introduced Brendan to Davoren. As far as I can remember, Brendan had no special magical line of access to Davoren. He didn't try any false (for him) moves of lifting or trying to romp with him. I think I write accurately when I recall the book-launch: to him, Davoren's handicaps were appalling.

But he was transfixed by Davoren's words, communications and poems. He didn't in fact meet Davoren that often. As I recall, he came only once to our house (I was a night-worker at the time) and they had a mixture of a roguish and serious chat. But for the remaining years of Davoren's and Brighid's lives he was unstinting in his support.

On the TV documentary made about Davoren, *Poised for Flight*, Brendan mentions Yeats and Davoren in the same breath as poets who honour friendship. When it comes to divining poetic promise *and* saying the truth as he sees it, Brendan is prepared to go out on a limb – not caring for academic protocols or niceties.

It was the same fearless and unabashed spirit which led him to describe Brighid as a mother who had lain down her life for her son at a reading organised by Poetry Ireland after her death. Brighid tried in every way she could to hang on to her own life – with her own health problems, she was living on the edge – but in the end she would battle on for Davoren, no matter what it cost her.

I sense a compelling mixture of reticence and outspokenness in Brendan. After first Brighid's death and then Davoren's four years later, Brendan had no public message to declaim: he was as stricken as the rest of us. I remember well, when he interviewed me for the *Arts Show* about a year after Brighid's death, feeling that Brendan was as baffled and at a loss as I.

But in other ways Brendan is a great subversive – wanting to break, and encouraging us all to break, the codes of silence and shyness in which we skulk away our feelings. He is no preacher; he leads by example. I meet him quite often on the streets. He tells me that he has pictures of Brigid and Davoren on the door to his room and that he often says 'hello' to them as he's going out. 'And they talk to me.' In the same unselfconscious way as he converses, rants and prays with Judas, Jesus and Cromwell in his poems, in his room he chats with Brighid and Davoren and they with him.

I conclude with a poem which Davoren wrote for Brendan after they first met in February 1985. It has the innocent adulatory quality which often found its way into Davoren's poetic addresses to people, but I am quite sure it captures something essential about that fount of encouragement, that sensitive being that is Brendan Kennelly.

Pleasure knew no bounds when we met
that grey-faced afternoon on the cobbles
of majestic learning's playground;
poetic language cannot describe
my fellow-feeling flight towards Danae
as I savoured your sensitive being.

MARIAL HANNON

Close Encounters of a Fourth Kind

What can one say about Professor Kennelly? One cannot say that
he is beautiful because he is ugly and one cannot say he is ugly
because he is beautiful. One cannot say he is kind because he is
cruel and one cannot say he is cruel because he is kind. One cannot say he is bright because he is dark and one cannot say he is
dark because he is bright. He is as Marx said of our age – preg-
nant with his own contrary.

I first met Professor Brendan Kennelly at the Hole in the Wall
theatre in Western Australia in 1988. At this time I was co-ordinating the tour of an exhibition of painting and sculpture from
artists working in the west of Ireland. I had called by to thank the
Chairman of the Yeats Society for their help in the presentation of
the 'West of Ireland Artists and Recent Irish Publications Exhibition'
which had opened earlier that week at the nearby State Library of
Western Australia. As the proceedings of the Yeats Society had
commenced, I was ushered in silence into the darkened auditorium. On stage I recognised Brendan Kennelly from his appearance
on the *Late Late Show* the previous year. He started to read his
translation of 'Caoineadh Airt Uí Laoghaire'. I was familiar with the
work from other readings. But now the words like heat seeking
missiles connected with the recognition of despair buried deep
and mostly out of reach in my media-age inured stomach. I was
glad the theatre was dark.

At coffee break, people emerged, shell-shocked it seemed to me
– they reminded me of kneaded pottery clay – they seemed suddenly aware of their plasticity and each one was a freshly thrown
vase. 'He is like God the Potter,' announced Shelly Rose, a dynamic
Australian woman who had travelled from Sydney to hear him
read. 'I have even travelled to Dublin on many occasions to hear
him read,' she informed me. I was amazed. 'But at the end of the
day,' she mused pragmatically as she sipped her tea, 'he is a typical spineless Irish man when it comes to women – it's the tragic
gap between art and life – the painter is not the picture – the poet
is not the poem.'

'Well what is he then?' I asked.

'I don't know – maybe he's a mystery.'

'Yes, that's it,' we concluded over tea and biscuits, 'he's a mystery and we can be happy to leave it at that. What do we want to

do?' Reduce what we have experienced to the timetable of elements – he is of the Aboriginal Dreaming – he can write, read, burp, roar, laugh, curse, stand up or lie down without being chased up and down suburbia by the butterfly catchers. He has to endure such suffering as a man with an itch that he can never scratch has to endure. That's it!' we volunteered generously, more for our own salvation than his, I felt. 'We will let him free from ourselves into The Dreaming – he is The Dreaming brushing our cheeks from the fourth or seventh dimension.'

The Irish Ambassador to Australia, James A. Sharkey, called me over and introduced me to Brendan Kennelly. 'Marial is here co-ordinating an exhibition of Irish art and an exhibition of recent Irish publications,' announced the Ambassador to the circle of tea drinkers. Kennelly eyed me quizzically. 'That's what we need!' he declared, 'somebody to do something for the poor poets. Do they know much about Irish writers out here?' he wanted to know.

'My experience is that Australians know a lot more about Irish writers than Irish artists,' I informed him.

'I hope you will have enough sense not to burn out your own gifts because it will be shit for thanks you will get at the end of the day – us writers and artists can be devils you know,' declared Kennelly in a nice yet paternalistic way. I was flabbergasted. The bystanders were awed.

The following year, back in Ireland, I was rushing towards Bewley's Coffee shop in Westmoreland Street, Dublin, with a folder of papers on the incoming Aboriginal Australian Utopia exhibition under my arm. Suddenly a figure stopped bolt upright in front of me in the street.

'Are you coming for the Tae?' asked Kennelly with a Listowel drawl.

'Ah sure I might as well,' I replied in my best County Clare accent. 'Why do you think we do that?' I asked – 'do this stage Irish mimicking of our own local dialects and ancestors?'

'Because we're ejits and fools,' replied Kennelly.

He was writing his *Book of Judas* at this time and was appearing on TV advertising Toyota cars.

'Lots of poets are horrified at you advertising cars on television,' I informed him.

'Ah fuck poets,' he replied, 'they know nothing. But some of them know how to drive!'

'Everybody blames Judas, you know,' he announced staring over his cup of coffee.

'You mean you think he is innocent?' I asked.

'We're all innocent,' he replied.

'We most certainly are not innocent,' I disagreed, 'we are all guilty as sin.'

'Oh the nuns have you got well and sure,' he sneered.

'Well, I would prefer to be under the spell of good and kind nuns than mesmerised by some boring egotistical ol' poet, painter or mouldy ol' rocker,' I responded narkily.

By the end of the coffee there was a form of consensus which recognised that we were all innocent, we were all guilty and we were all virgins.

'Would you sleep with me?' he asked with a mixture of suspicion and curiosity. 'I would not,' I replied emphatically.

'I suppose you are waiting for Mr Right,' he sneered.

'I don't believe in Mr Right,' I said,' it's just that I just think of myself as a Temple of the Holy Spirit.'

'Doesn't stop you stuffing yourself with buns though!' he retorted.

'No it doesn't but that is different – I think,' I laughed. 'I suppose you think that I am suffering from illusions of grandeur?'

'No, I do not think you are suffering from illusions of grandeur,' he said pensively – 'if more people knew that they were temples of the Holy Spirit they might be nicer to themselves and each other and there would be less blackness. I went to Mass today, and there was this priest rattling off prayers and flinging the host at us, with all the spirituality of a duck. Sometimes I think they do not believe in the Transubstantiation at all.'

'Maybe the priest does believe in the Transubstantiation,' I proposed, 'but maybe somedays he just cannot make it – cannot connect and falls to Earth like that angel in one of your poems – like the girl on the tightrope walking a road between Heaven and Earth, between God and gravity. Somedays she doubts herself and falls off and then she tries again and makes it across.'

'Priests and priestesses are on a tightrope and the grounded bogbillies are hell-bent on bringing them to Earth so ate grass, drink beer and bonk alongside themselves. People apart irritate others you know,' Kennelly concluded.

Two years later, in 1993, I was working at the Siamsa Tíre Theatre and Arts Centre in Tralee, County Kerry. One of the projects I initiated was based on the 'Utopia – A Picture Story Project' from Australia. Children from the Kerry/Cork region together with children in Poland, Germany and Sweden were invited to document stories from elderly persons living in their localities. I had invited Professor Kennelly to write the catalogue introduction and he had also agreed to come down and perform the official opening on Easter Weekend as part of the Samhaiocht Chiarraí Festival. The opening was to be followed by a reading by Kennelly in the theatre later that evening which he had titled 'The Resurrection of the Dead'.

I walked to Tralee train station to meet the professor from the Dublin train. It was a ten-minute walk. It was a bright but cool day.

'How are you getting on down here among this lot ?' he asked.

'Oh you will be delighted to hear that your old friend Judas is kept well busy – there are so many pins in my back now that I am bracing myself for martyrdom like St Sebastian,' I replied laughing.

'That's because you have a great gift,' he replied kindly, 'and gifts make the begrudgers jealous.'

'Do you know what they say up in Clare about that?' I asked.

'They say, motor on Macduff and fuck the begrudgers!'

'They can't touch you,' he said.

'You are right – they can't!' I exclaimed, grateful for this momentary cosmic perspective on myself.

'Motor on Macduff and fuck the begrudgers!!' he bellowed from the top of Ashe Street, much to everybody's amazement.

Hundreds of children, parents, grandparents and neighbours came for the opening. Kennelly climbed up on the wooden boxes and podium set up in the Town Park and riveted the air – exhorting the children, students and parents, politicians, councillors, teachers and business people to forget the shackles of stultifying respectability – to be creative and alive and to nurture the great women in their midst. He had the presence of a prophet and spoke like a philosopher – yet he was as if in his own room. He was loved and begrudged simultaneously by his fellow county people and he enjoyed every moment and nuance of the situation. 'And if you ever get into Government,' he exhorted Dick Spring, then the leader of the opposition Labour Party, from his height – 'don't forget to do something for the poor old arts.' 'Oh ye will have a long wait!' quipped one Fianna Fáil councillor and everybody laughed uproariously.

Descending from his podium, Kennelly gathered all the children in the gallery with their stories and art works and made them sit on the floor. He stood in the middle of the floor and began telling them the story of the spinning clown. Suddenly, to the delight of the children and the amazement of the assembled parents and councillors, he was down on the floor on his hands and knees and rolling over on top of his head. 'Christ almighty but he knows no bounds at all,' said Seanie Mahony, one of the Siamsa Tíre performers.

'Your "Resurrection of the Dead" is booked out for this evening in the theatre,' I informed Kennelly. He was delighted. 'They love me and they hate me, you know, and sometimes they don't know the difference. It will be the resurrection of the dead all right before I'm finished with them!' he said vehemently.

'You know how you are always going on about Education and access and the point system and the stifling of creativity?' I ventured. 'Well would you be one to do a short reading at the Abbey Inn pub after the theatre this evening?'

'I will if you want,' he said.

The Abbey Inn is known mainly as a bikers' pub in Tralee though its patrons are many and varied but all are young. Danny Leane, the proprietor, was one of the first to agree to sponsor the 'Resurrection of the Dead' poster for the reading. Many young people there would never dream of going to a reading at the Siamsa Tíre which they told me was only for doctors' daughters and rich people's children to learn diddle eie. Even though this was far from the truth, this perception was very strong and Kennelly agreed that it would be a great idea to try out a reading in the pub.

That evening Kennelly started his reading at the plush Siamsa Tíre Theatre at 8.30 p.m. to a packed auditorium. 'How do you think it is going?' he asked me nervously at the interval, as we brought him a glass of water in his dressing room. 'It is going absolutely brilliantly,' I reassured him somewhat taken aback that he would be so nervous and insecure. The whole audience are now out in the foyer and they are trying to make more seats available for people still trying to get in.

By the time the book signing was completed after the reading, it was 10.40 pm before we left for the Abbey Inn. 'Are you sure you are able for this?' I asked.

'I am flying it!' he replied as he belted up the street before us.

The Abbey Inn was packed to the doors. The bouncer, one of the No Hopers Bikers group, welcomed us jumping forward to shake hands with Kennelly and usher us through the throng at the door. A crescendo of heavy metal, cigarette smoke and shouting met us. Leane waded towards us. 'Jesus!' groaned Kennelly, 'are we going to be bottled here or what?'

'Keep the cool,' I whispered loudly back – 'just remember this is where U2 did one of their first gigs and Danny got them to sweep up the floor afterwards – it's in Bono's autobiography.

'Well he can bloody do his own sweeping tonight!' retorted Kennelly.

On stage in full regalia was a five-piece metal band, Paul and

Urban Gipsy, from Ballymun in Dublin, fronted by the lead singer draped in a Japanese flag. Danny Leane warmly shook Kennelly's hand. 'We thought you were only having us on – hang on a minute till I tell the band – they are expecting you.' Urban Gipsy stopped in full flight and took to their seats in the wings. Kennelly took the stage. 'If he survives this,' pronounced Padraig Kennelly Senior, the Editor of the *Kerry's Eye* newspaper, who had enthroned himself at the bar, 'it really is "The Resurrection of the Dead"!'

Kennelly stepped on stage amid a cloud of cigarette smoke and with a dozen nonchalant teenagers sitting on the ground looking at him, somewhat derisory. But the instance he spoke an amazing stillness enveloped the assembly. Holding aloft *Moloney Up and At It* he launched into the bawdy ballads celebrating the vicissitudes of lust and middle age. The audience loved it.

Then, in an instance, as if he was a brilliant magician, we were transported to the full colour of the circus, gazing breathlessly at the girl on the tightrope:

> And the village children
> Stare at the girl on the tightrope
> As if they were astronauts
> Staring at the world
> Like men on the first morning of creation
> Seeing mountains valleys rivers lakes
> In colours never seen before...
>
> She is stepping a line
> The children have never known
> Somewhere between earth and sky
> Somewhere they have never been
>
> A line of danger and adventure
> A line of longing and of love
> A line of breathing and of breathlessness
> A line of poised humanity and vigilant divinity.
>
> ('Girl on a Tightrope')

In the next instance he had taken them from their laughter and joy almost to the edge of tears with 'Caoineadh Airt Uí Laoghaire'.

The stillness of almost two hundred people was remarkable. Pints stood untouched and cigarettes, I noticed, began to grow long tails of ash as the glow spread menacingly towards rigidly held fingers. People knew they were witnessing the extraordinary. There was a sense of being a participant in a fleeting moment of incandescence – like seeing a meteor streak across the sky, knowing that its brilliance was sourced in a world and time far from your own.

In the final ovation of cheering bikers and cheering non-bikers, Kennelly, tired yet carried by the crowd, finished the night:

What is this room
But the moments we have lived in it?
When all due has been paid
To Gods of wood and stone
And recognition has been made
Of those who'll breathe here when we are gone
Does it not take its worth from us
Who made it because we were here?...

We are living
In ceiling, floor and windows,
We are given to where we have been.
This white door will always open
On what our hands have touched
Our eyes have seen.

('We Are Living')

Professor Brendan Kennelly at the Abbey Inn, with members of Urban
Gipsy in the background (photo: Kerry Kennelly, *Kerry's Eye*)

CHARLES J. HAUGHEY

Launch of Brendan Kennelly's *Poetry My Arse* in the AIB Banking Hall, College Street, Dublin, 25 September 1995

To launch a new book is always interesting; to launch a book of new poetry is exciting; to launch a book of new poetry by Professor Brendan Kennelly is a happening of significance.

This is Brendan Kennelly's third epic poem. The first was *Cromwell*, the second was *The Book of Judas*. Though both of these dealt with historical figures, they also succeeded in being relevant and contemporary and in telling us a great deal about the world we live in today.

This epic poem follows along the same pathway. This time, however, the focus is very much on the Dublin of our time. He tries to capture the essence of the city and to describe its character: It looks at our lifestyles, what we talk about, what we are amused by, scandalised by, afraid of, inspired by.

It is about a poet Ace de Horner and his lover Janey Mary. The phonetic relationship of the poet's name with one of our major cultural institutions is surely a coincidence.

The title of the book, *Poetry My Arse*, is as original as it is intriguing. The intention is to bring out another edition especially for the intelligentsia of Europe which will be entitled *La Poésie mon Cul*. At a later stage there will be a special Irish edition entitled *Filíocht, mo Thóin*.

Brendan Kennelly is a people's poet and very much a poet of our time. He is passionately involved with people and their concerns. He writes about us and for us, observing with great sympathy and understanding the different aspects of our everyday lives: joy, sorrow, pain, hardship, love, sex, loneliness, success, failure, hope. Brendan's poetry is a great tide of ideas, insights, feelings and experiences flowing all around us and pushing into every corner of our existence. He is truly Shakespearean in his great, sweeping, comprehensive coverage of the entire human condition.

His poetry has great range, scope and versatility. Take for instance his delightful little book of poems from the Irish, *Love of Ireland*; here we have a collection of poems full of beautiful imagery and descriptions of nature and wildlife and the sea, very different from the robust style of, say, *The Book of Judas*.

Brendan Kennelly loves his own poetry. He delights in it. He glories in reciting it from memory; word-perfect; verse after verse pouring out like a waterfall cascading down the mountainside.

This is a funny poem. It is a sad poem. It is a thoughtful poem. I believe it will help us to see clearly what is happening around us and to think equally clearly about what we see and then hopefully to understand it all a little better. If it does that, Brendan Kennelly will be well satisfied.

Poets come in all sorts of shapes and sizes, with different attitudes and demeanours. This one here this evening is a very special version of the species – a penetrating intellect, combined with keen observation; a man full of wisdom, compassion and laughter; brilliant conversationalist and boon companion; all in all a lovable individual person whose latest work I now with great relish launch on an unsuspecting Irish public.

From Flattery to Fellowship

One Christmas when I was ten years old, I was given a collection of short stories and poems as a present. While reading the book I came across a poem entitled 'Poem from a Three Year Old'. Prior to this, in school we had only been exposed to simple, happy, childlike poems. This poem was the first poem that I remember making me feel sad and that started me thinking beyond my simple day to day routine. This was my first encounter with the work of Brendan Kennelly.

Little did I know that in just over two years I would meet this poet in person. I used to write some poetry now and then at the time and some twenty or thirty poems had accumulated. In the summer of 1990, when I was twelve, my father announced that we were going to a poetry reading by Brendan Kennelly. He told me to gather up some of my favourite poems which I had written, and bring them along with a letter about myself, that I could give to Brendan Kennelly at the end.

What evolved that evening took me very much by surprise. After the reading, when the audience was offered the chance to ask questions, my Dad whispered to me, telling me to ask him when he wrote his first poem. The question was purposely chosen, because when I asked he replied: 'When did you write yours?' Before I knew it he had the envelope I had planned to give him *after* the reading, and was hijacking it by reading out my poetry to the audience.

I was twelve years old, extremely embarrassed and ready to kill my father. But in retrospect, I know that at the same time I was very flattered by the praise he had showered on my poems. It was the first time anyone had ever publicly commented on my poetry. After the reading, he gave me a signed copy of his current book of poetry, *A Time for Voices*, and said he would be in touch. Within three days he rang me, inviting me out for dinner with him sometime, and to tell me again how impressed he was.

Dinner never happened and because I was so caught up with starting secondary school, I never wrote either. After a few years I assumed he would have forgotten about me altogether. To my surprise, however, in September 1994 he met my father again, and asked about me. I could not believe that he actually remembered me from four years previously. Not long after, I wrote to him and I sent him some of my more recent poetry. Within days he rang me to thank me for writing to him. He continued to say that he liked my poems a lot, even though he did find them quite sad, and that they reminded him of the work of George Herbert. A letter followed, full of encouragement to keep on writing, and a present of a book of Herbert's poems. I was very touched by his personal response to my letter and genuine interest in and encouragement of me and my work.

I have read a certain amount of his poetry and studied one or two poems for the Junior Certificate, and must admit that I liked them all. The one that I especially like is 'Poem from a Three Year Old', which made such an impression on me at a young age. I have no qualification or authority to judge his work in literary terms and standards, but I do know that I personally like it. I admire him as a poet but even more so for his personal response and interest in me when first I met him, and when I contacted him again. I was very touched by how he went so far out of his way to contact me, encourage me and talk to me about my poetry. One thing that particularly impressed me was how when he talked to me he did not talk down to me, but spoke to me as an equal about my poetry, even though I was a sixteen-year-old schoolgirl.

Benison for Brendan

I *Brendan at Bouillargues*

The reek of kerosene soiled the night air,
But the high summertime of the Gard
Was warm and welcoming everywhere.
Travellers debouched from Air Inter's caravelle.
Excited by the foreign ambience of Nîmes,
Brendan strode swiftly across the tarmac,
Radiant, ebullient, his eyes gleaming.

We drove to the fête at Bouillargues,
Jeanne and I in charge of Lédenon's young,
Expected to drink, though mainly they clung
Close through those interminably long dances,
Swaying to the voice of young Mireille Mattieu
Echoing, battering across the village square.

Brendan took in the fête with swift glances,
Asked for change, to fire at the dancing ball
Which he hit each time with a single shot
Out of the crooked barrel of the rifle,
Viewed amazedly the champagne he'd got,
The applause of the local lads and girls.
He moved on to a machine you struck
To prove your power, and won there too,
Repeatedly, modestly saying 'I'm in luck.'

The bottles were brought to our table,
Tucked in the dark corner of the square,
While Brendan explored the fun of the fair:
Nothing he could not win, for he was able
Through strength and skill to win at all
These sideshows, a hero quite invincible –
Until his mere approach caused each stall
To be scuttled, shuttered down and locked.

He gave bottles to gypsies, any passer-by,
Everyone drank and everyone was high;
We loaded the car with the champagne,

And Brendan went off to hunt again
For any stall that would stand up to him;
But not many did, nor could: he'd won
Champagne on a scale that would overbrim
Any Gaelic epic of excess, and the fun
Of that fair enveloped him like a halo.
His thighs flamed, with a salmon leap he lofted
Across the sounding square, every girl there
Seeing the poet in the man, his brave soul elate,
Reflected in sparkling eyes beneath that curling hair:
Brendan *Og*, released from misty Irish air
Into the moonlit brilliance of Bouillargues fair.

II *Brendan's Great Gift*

Your memory menaces, ready to pounce
From the bushes that have concealed it;
Revealing sheer strength, you can denounce,
By implication, those who have a deficit,
Who walk the jungle tracks of conversation
Nervously inadequate, looking over their shoulders,
Unable to match your copious quotation,
Nodding agreement, nothing in memory's folders
To allow them to face you on equal terms
A thing your knowingly innocent face confirms.

III *Brendan the Sharer*

With Brendan one can collaborate;
And that's a very searching test
Of anyone, on which I won't elaborate,
Except to say I value the zest
He brings to the final deliberate
Judgements of what is in or out,
For he is a man born to cooperate.
We both relish the knockabout,
Kindred, perhaps, in temperament;
Both serious, open to amusement,
We enjoy sharing out our enjoyment.

IV *Brendan, Humane Scholar*

Brendan is a good examiner,
Which is to say that he assesses
Not only what is written down or said,
But the potential the person possesses.
His standards are impeccable;
But he can see merit, and is led
To explore and find the discoverable
Excellences. He is an encourager
Of a shy student in a viva, showing
The genuine depth of his interest
In the nature of their thought, knowing
That once this is made manifest
They will demonstrate their ability,
Responding to his true liberality.

V *Brendan the Poet*

Brendan in Leeds, apparently an academic
In the making, reading, writing a thesis,
For knowledge hydroptic, yet still a romantic,
The serious approach as yet a hypothesis.
Barrel-bodied, taut-muscled, he'd enter the Eldon –
The sort of night he'd describe eventually
As one on which you'd gleefully abandon
Discretion: puck a fellow, unzip a barmaid,
Or, on the way home, effortlessly uproot a tree,
In the morning seem entirely sober and staid.
Some of this is hidden in an early, slender novel;
But his imagination was far freer than fiction;
He needed the precision of poetry, to marvel
At mankind and at all human contradiction.
Cruelty he saw, and described in harsh detail
To exorcise haunting images of pain and blood:
Pigs killed, bulls castrated, the strong cocktail
Shaken, the bitters added: countryman as stud,
Girl's love-cry echoing over the Kerry hills,
Black foxes gnawing at dark fathers' vitals:
All this cascades over pages till it fills
The memories of others; but rough recitals
Purge the poet, liberate him and exorcise

59

These affronts to sensibility; and enable,
Brief capture, a sudden glimpse of paradise –
The lyric joy of beauty, at once so vulnerable
And yet so lasting. History next for exploring,
Cromwell to ponder over in his Englishness:
His bloody progress but a successful whoring
After strange gods, unlike the heathenishness
That Cromwell, despite Patrick's work, was deploring
In a way that the poet felt required exploring;
Just as he felt, surgeon-like, that the pancreas,
The lights, the liver, the urbane predestined
Kiss should be removed, until Judas
Beneath his sharpened scalpel lay eviscerated,
But surrounded by the operating theatre's crew,
Jesus a detached observer of Kennelly's wit,
The other characters there knowing what to do –
Demask, wash up, drink up, and then fit
Themselves into Toyotas to drive into the night,
For they are no longer needed, are superseded
By a violent crew that blaze into the daylight,
Stage light, too, under which they've speeded,
Their tragic passion at the wheel, the mistake
In steering their course fatal, Greeks by name,
But universal through the years: no brake
Can stop them; and no one really to blame;
His translations show us we're just the same.

JOHN B. KEANE

The Bard of Ballylongford

I well recall my first meeting with Brendan Kennelly. It was in the family pub in Ballylongford. He was in his early teens, with a cherub face and a great ear for poetry.

I remember it was the first time I was ever addressed as 'Mister'. A huge Ballylongford man by the name of Tim Sullivan stretched out his hand and said: 'You are welcome to Ballylongford, Mr Keane.' He bought me a pint of stout into the bargain.

Kennelly was there behind the counter with his beautiful mother, she was Ahern herself, a sister of Ger Ahern's of Ballyline. She was calm and gracious with an unforgettable gentility.

I knew Brendan had an ear for poetry by the way he listened. When I quoted *The Song of Wandering Aengus* he listened intently, as indeed did most of the people there on that occasion. He willed them to listen.

At that first meeting he quoted one of his poems which delighted all present. It was a short poem and the sort of jingle you would expect from a teenager was absent. There was a rare maturity in his work even then. As he spoke he seemed to be in the process of celebrating life.

I remember meeting him some years later when he was in his late teens. It was on Carrig Island where he had been bathing. It was a lovely summer's day and we spoke for a long while about poetry and then, too, there was the same excitement, the same vibrancy and vitality as he sought to embrace life.

Again I got the impression that here was a man bent on celebrating every hour he was given. Nobody values the gift of life more than Brendan. I know of no man with the same regard for this gift and he can infuse other people with his enthusiasm for life.

He is a product of Ballylongford, called by some people a village, other people call it The Cross. I have always called Ballylongford a town, albeit a small town, but a town, nevertheless, with all the characteristics of a town and all the characters, with its own river and the sea beyond.

It is a most civilised place and I am happy to be able to say that I have never left that lovely spot in a sober state, having availed myself of the wares available in the many fine hostelries which are strung out along its streets.

Among his contemporaries Kennelly shines out. He is a sort of mixture between Yeats and Kavanagh comprising the best of both. In his selection of poems, *A Time for Voices: Selected Poems 1960-1990*, are to be found the many voices of Kennelly. Here we can see the influence of Yeats and Kavanagh but yet here is a very singular voice which owes nothing really to anybody, except to Kennelly's spiritual and geographical origins and, of course, to his own people.

He is the very soul of the village where he was born – Ballylongford. He is its narrator. He is its confessor. He has taken that village into his heart and given us a look at the souls of its people. He loves the place and the people of Ballylongford love him in return.

He is loved, above all, by women and he is blessed with some outrageous dimples which still break hearts, even now, and but for his natural sexual restraint those dimples would have been imposed on thousands of Irish children. Women, wanton and willing, women wise and wary woo him from morning till night.

Kennelly has this particular restraint which keeps women at bay. He has a detachment as well in dealing with them. He loves women but there is always that detachment which commits him to observations and appreciation rather than seduction.

I always found in Kennelly an intense warmth and concern for others, but there was always, too, a distance between himself and reality. It seems to me that in that little space between the poet and the people who live around him there is an exclusive area where he forms his personal interpretations of the antics, the idiosyncrasies, the struggles and the loneliness of his people.

He has a total understanding but he needs that space between himself and those about whom he writes in order to embellish, or to substance or to flesh them out properly and he does it admirably.

If the volume *A Time for Voices* is his entire life's work, if he had never written anything else, if he had never written *The Book of Judas* or all the other fine poems, this book would qualify him as one of Ireland's finest poets. To me it shows Kennelly as a great poet and I find that I can dip into this volume at any time. There are 176 poems in the book and of those I would say that at least 100 are memorable.

Another great quality of Kennelly's poetry which is rarely found these days is that all his lines fall very gently on the ear. It is very easy to memorise Kennelly. I know that everybody will not agree with me but poetry that lends itself to memory is the only poetry that endures.

I always found that all the great poets I read going to school forced themselves upon me without my almost knowing it. The same can be said of Kennelly's poems.

I remember once for his birthday I recited his poem 'I See You Dancing, Father' on Radio Éireann; I also remember his father.

It was at an election meeting in Ballylongford and Brendan's father climbed onto a platform with my uncle Mick Purtill, who was his friend, and other members of the Fine Gael party.

First he turned around and tapping the floor with his small feet he said to my uncle Mick, 'A lovely platform for a dance Mick,' and he gave us a little dance before the actual meeting started.

I See You Dancing, Father

No sooner downstairs after the night's rest
And in the door
Than you started to dance a step
In the middle of the kitchen floor.

As you danced
You whistled.
You made your own music
Always in tune with yourself.

Well, nearly always, anyway.
You're buried now
In Lislaughtin Abbey
And whenever I think of you

I go back beyond the old man
Mind and body broken
To find the unbroken man.
It is the moment before the dance begins,

Your lips are enjoying themselves
Whistling an air.
Whatever happens or cannot happen
In the time I have to spare
I see you dancing, father.

Now there is a beautiful poem. It tells us an awful lot about Brendan, as do all his poems, but this one in particular tells me about the vulnerability of the man. In this poem there is concern, love and anguish – the anguish of memory and compassion.

I remember him as a footballer. I met him in the 1954 North Kerry championship semi-final in which Ballylongford beat us by a point. He had played with the Kerry minors in that same year and played very well.

I remember when my own son, John, played against Dublin in the 1980 All-Ireland Minor Football Final, Kerry were beaten by a point.

That night Brendan Kennelly rang John up and spoke to him for an hour, consoling him, telling him of his own feelings of despondency and despair when they were also beaten by the same score by Dublin in another All-Ireland Minor final.

I remember that John's despondency vanished and he went out that night and celebrated as he never celebrated before. Kennelly has this uncanny ability to help people, to help them back on the road of life and to chart a true course for them.

He has, many a time, charted a course for myself, but I know that it is very hard to chart a course for a man with a mule-like disposition like myself, but he has partially succeeded. One of my great regrets is that I have not paid more attention to what he has said to me.

I remember one time when we were both drinking whiskey, we had consumed about a bottle each. It was in our respective heydays when nothing in the world seemed to matter except whiskey. Afterwards when he was on his way to Ballylongford, I walked up the Clieveragh Road with him and we came across a horse looking out over a gate. Kennelly stopped and spoke to the horse. There followed one of the most engaging, silly and fantastic conversations, well, one-sided conversations, to which I ever listened.

First of all he harangued the horse and told him that he should not be leaning out over gates looking at people. Then he went on to eulogise the horse. By the time we had finished the horse had turned into an enchanted horse.

We both had a difficult time with drink and as a result we have a better understanding of each other's problems but we have both conquered drink. Brendan does not drink at all now and I have so arranged my life that it is not necessary for me to drink at all if I choose, but I do drink on occasion and I have great control over it.

He had beautiful parents. He comes from a family of eight children. He has two sisters and five brothers. The girls were talented and lovely and the brothers all footballers to a man and all with talent waiting there to be used.

The Kennellys had a peculiar style of football, nobody more so than Brendan. They were the best free takers in North Kerry and that is saying something, because North Kerry was a great place for free takers.

It was Kennelly's approach to a ball that set him apart. He had a knack of taking on the most capricious of breezes. To flight a ball properly when there is a swirling wind is an almost impossible achievement, but he had this knack.

There was poetry in his movement when he came to kick a point from a placed ball. I have lost count of the times I have seen him kick great points from frees, effect great clearances from a free or from his hands. He had a mighty drive of a ball.

One of the things I will always remember about him is the way he would loft his head in the air and look quizzically upwards as if listening for intimations from the prevailing breeze or wind.

When he found out what he wanted to know, he would bend his head and look solemnly down at the ball, look up once more briefly, withdraw and then trot and then run before he struck the ball to flight it beautifully without regard for wind, rain or any other element.

Finally, I would wish that he would write more short poems because it is here that he excels. I would wish that he would write another *Book of Judas* and I would wish him a long, long life full of laughter and the voices of women circling him and protecting him and weaving magic spells about his hair-bedecked ears. Farewell a while sweet prince of poetry, bright shining, dimpled bard of Ballylongford.

Voices from Galway

1

ÅP: 'If I say Brendan Kennelly, what do you say?'
Woman 1: 'I've heard of him.'
ÅP: 'In what capacity?'
Woman 1: 'He's a critic, in newspapers.'
ÅP: 'Mainly newspapers?'
Woman 1: 'Yes, but I've seen him on the telly, I think it was on the *Late Late Show*.'
ÅP: 'If I say that he's a poet, does that ring a bell?'
Woman 1: 'No.'
ÅP: 'Thank you.'

2

ÅP: 'Do you recognise the name Brendan Kennelly?'
Woman 2: 'Should I?'
ÅP: 'I'm just wondering. You haven't heard of him?'
Woman 2: 'No, not at all, sorry.'
ÅP: 'Thanks.'

3

ÅP: 'Do you know Brendan Kennelly?'
Woman 3: 'Yes, I do.'
ÅP: 'How?'
Woman 3: 'I've often heard him on the radio, seen him on television, on the *Late Late*.'
ÅP: 'Is that how you have encountered him?'
Woman 3: 'It would be, yes.'
ÅP: 'Have you read any of his works?'
Woman 3: 'No, but I've read some of his articles in the papers, but I haven't bought any books, poetry or anything like that.'
ÅP: 'So you've seen him mainly in the media?'
Woman 3: 'Yes. Including his ads!'
ÅP: 'Including his ads? You've heard his ads?'
Woman 3: 'Yes, on the Toyota cars.'
ÅP: 'Thank you.'

4

ÅP: 'Brendan Kennelly, have you heard that name?'
Man 1: 'Indeed I have.'
ÅP: 'How?'
Man 1: 'Well, he's a Professor of English at TCD, he's a poet, he does the adverts for Toyota, that's it.'
ÅP: 'Have you read anything?'
Man 1: 'Hm, not recently, some of his stuff, way back.
ÅP: 'Where have you seen him?'
Man 1: 'I don't know, really, I suppose TV coverage, or radio.'
ÅP: 'Not his poetry?'
Man 1: 'No, not really, no, I'm not really big into poetry as such, but, well, my brother is, so it could also have been through him, I suppose.
ÅP: 'OK, that's all, thank you.'

5

ÅP: 'Have you heard of Brendan Kennelly?'
Man 2: 'I have.'
ÅP: 'How have you heard of him?'
Man 2: 'I've heard of him in a number of ways. Number one, he's a lecturer in the university, number two, he's a poet, and then, of course, he does the Toyota ads.'
ÅP: 'Where did you first hear of him?'
Man 2: 'Through his poetry.'
ÅP: 'Have you read any of his poetry?'
Man 2: 'I've read some of his poems, yes.'
ÅP: 'Early? Later?'
Man 2: 'Hm, various types of poems. I've known about him for quite some time.'
ÅP: 'So you would definitely recognise him?'
Man 2: Oh, no problem. But I've never actually met him or seen the man in the flesh, but I've seen him on the *Late Late Show*.'
ÅP: 'Thank you.'

6

ÅP: 'Do you know who Brendan Kennelly is?'
Woman 4: 'Brendan Kennelly? Hm, yes, I think so. I can't remember exactly what, but I think so, yes. It rings a bell.'
ÅP: 'A writer?'
Woman 4: 'He's a poet! Poet, yes, poet.'

67

ÅP: 'Anything else?'

Woman 4: 'Maybe there was something about alcohol, maybe.'

ÅP: 'Where was that?'

Woman 4: 'On the TV, or on the *Late Late* or something. I've heard him read his poetry, you know on television he read a few poems, but I haven't read any, myself.'

ÅP: 'OK, thank you.'

7

ÅP: 'Brendan Kennelly, do you recognise that name?'

Woman 5: 'Yes.'

ÅP: 'In what ways have you heard of him?'

Woman 5: 'Hm, he's a lecturer, in Trinity College. I've seen him on television, in the papers, in the news.'

ÅP: 'Are you familiar with his work?'

Woman 5: 'No, I haven't read any. Regrettably. But he's very entertaining, very enjoyable to listen to.'

ÅP: 'All right, thank you.'

8

ÅP: 'Brendan Kennelly, have you heard of him?'

Woman 6: 'Yes.'

ÅP: 'How?'

Woman 6: 'He's a poet.'

ÅP: 'Have you read anything by him?'

Woman 6: 'Short extracts, but I don't have any books. Actually, I think I've seen him once, in Boston. He read in Boston. It was Brendan Kennelly, wasn't it? I think it was him, anyway.

ÅP: 'Have you seen him anywhere else?'

Woman 6: 'I've seen him on television a couple of times, on one of the chat-shows, the *Late Late* or something like that. I've also seen him mentioned in the papers, maybe in connection with his books or something, that's about it.'

ÅP: 'OK, thank you.'

9

ÅP: 'Are you familiar with Brendan Kennelly?'

Man 3: 'No.'

ÅP: 'Not at all?'

Man 3: 'No.'

ÅP: 'Thank you.'

10

ÅP: 'If I say Brendan Kennelly, what do you say?'
Woman 7: 'The poet, yes, I've heard of him.'
ÅP: 'Do you know his work?'
Woman 7: 'Just some of it. I taught a few of his poems to children preparing for speech and drama exams.'
ÅP: 'His early poetry, or later?'
Woman 7: 'Oh, I'd say it would be his earlier poems, but I haven't read much about him, except perhaps an article in the *Times* now and again. I don't know an awful lot about him, I know he's very popular, senior pupils like his work.'
ÅP: 'Thanks.'

11

ÅP: 'Do you know Brendan Kennelly?'
Woman 8: 'Yes.'
ÅP: 'How do you know him?'
Woman 8: 'Well, he's in Trinity, he's an English teacher in Trinity. And I know him from television, and I know he doesn't drive! I've also heard him on the radio, he's been interviewed a few times.'
ÅP: 'When did you first hear of him?'
Woman 8: 'Oh, a long time ago.'
ÅP: 'All right, thank you.'

12

ÅP: 'Have you heard of Brendan Kennelly?'
Man 4: 'Brendan Kennelly? Eh, yes, he's a poet.'
ÅP: 'Have you read any of his work?'
Man 4: 'No, I'm not into poetry.'
ÅP: 'Is that the only thing you've heard of him?'
Man 4: 'He advertises some kind of car on television. Since I don't drive it doesn't make that much difference what kind of car he's driving.'
ÅP: 'Any other places you've seen him or heard of him?'
Man 4: 'No.'
ÅP: 'When would you have heard of him first?'
Man 4: 'I don't know, somewhere around 1945, I suppose.'
ÅP: '1945? How did you know him then?'
Man 4: 'I wouldn't remember, but I might have heard of him then, 'cos that's when we got our radio, 1945.'

ÅP: 'He would have been quite young then?'

Man 4: 'Maybe, I don't know, it makes no difference to me.'

ÅP: 'OK, thank you.'

13

ÅP: 'Brendan Kennelly, is he familiar to you?'

Man 5: 'Yes, he's a poet who advertises Toyota motor cars.'

ÅP: 'Did you hear of him first as a poet or advertiser?'

Man 5: 'Hm, probably as a poet, but I have to say I would associate him more with Toyota.'

ÅP: 'Have you seen him in any other media?'

Man 5: 'No, only in the Toyota ads, on the radio. But I haven't read anything by him. My wife is interested in literature, so she reads a lot of poetry, I'm more into mathematics, so...'

ÅP: 'Thank you.'

14

ÅP: 'Brendan Kennelly, have you heard of him?'

Man 6: 'Mm.'

ÅP: 'How?'

Man 6: 'I've seen him on the telly, but I haven't read any of his books, but I know about him, yes.'

ÅP: 'So you know he's a writer?'

Man 6: 'Sure. I'd love to meet that guy, actually, I was thinking about him only a couple of months ago, that I would like to meet him, just because of his humanitarian sort of spirit. I've heard him on the radio recently, I'm very impressed with the way he thinks, straight, direct, as I say, his humanitarian sort of way, that's the way I can describe it.'

ÅP: 'Have you read anything?'

Man 6: 'I've picked up a book now and then and read the odd poem, but I haven't bought any books.'

ÅP: 'Thanks.'

15

ÅP: 'Does the name Brendan Kennelly say anything to you?'

Woman 9: 'Brendan Kenneally? Kenneally?'

ÅP: 'Kennelly.'

Woman 9: 'Kennelly? No.'

ÅP: 'Doesn't ring a bell at all?'

Woman 9: 'Kennelly? Comedian? No, I'm afraid not.'

ÅP: 'Thank you.'

SISTER STANISLAUS KENNEDY

Brendan Kennelly: Kerryman and Poet

Brendan Kennelly is a writer of great clarity and assurance and he has a vision of hope. But as well as looking forward with hope, he also has a gift for memory, remembering with faithfulness, and his poetry is a validation of his deep bond with his homeplace, Kerry, which is my homeplace also. He has a great sense of place in his writing and in his talk. He has never forgotten his Kerry roots, and I honour him for that.

Kennelly's poetry is an account of a straightforward search for a life connected with the soil, with humanity and with whatever is spiritual. He writes with determination and faithfulness of values that endure, of nature, the family, the community, caring, compassion, justice, tradition. His poems shine with the wisdom of somebody who has thought deeply about the paradoxical strangeness and familiarity and wonder of life. He has a special gift for making the ordinary extraordinary, and for making the extraordinary ordinary. You can read a poem of his, and suddenly the words have new meanings, and you see new things in the world around you.

He can write about exalted topics and make them accessible and everyday, and he can write about the everyday and turn these things into the stuff of poetry. In his early poetry, particularly, he writes about the things we take for granted, familiar things, as even a quick review of some of his titles reveals – 'The Pig Killer', 'The Thatcher', 'The Gift', 'The Island', 'Lightning', 'Islandman', 'Water' – and he turns these simple things into poetry. Water, for instance, he describes as:

> Chuckling in gutters,
> Active in the corner field
> Or barely bending the slightest flowers
>
> Its pace is perfect.
> Bridge between earth and sky,
> Lucid contract
>
> Between all things that wish to grow...

This wonderful poem ends:

> Laughter down the side of a hill,
> A playful rumpus at
> The doorway, the freckled thrill

> On the river's face; and I marvel again
> At the presence that lives
> Because it is gone.

Brendan Kennelly is a spiritual poet. He can put us in touch with that place within ourselves described by Thomas Martin as being 'the still point, that centre within us where God's name is written'. He speaks with the voice of 'Silence' when he says:

> Once I was the heartbeat of the world
> But am an outcast now.
> Why did you find it so difficult
>
> To live with me?...
> I will be speechless when I wait for you
> For when I speak, I'm lost.

We are all experts at building shells around ourselves, so that we cease to be aware of what is going on within us and around us, but to grow to our full beauty we need to have those shells broken frequently, so that the sun and the air and the water can get in and enable us to grow. And that is what I believe Brendan Kennelly does. He touches the heart of the matter and the heart of our being. He breaks our shells and lets in the light.

In fact, he himself talks about this in his Preface to one of his early volumes of poetry, *Selected Poems* (1969), where he says:

> I believe that each one of us is blind in a great number of ways; and that saves us. I believe that occasionally we see things in our blindness ...We are cripplingly limited. To recognise this is a strength. To celebrate it is to discover a kind of indestructibility, to achieve definition...

Isn't that wonderful! You could think about that and meditate on it all your life. You could pray about that all your life and try to grow into that definition that is always changing. That for me is the meaning of spirituality and the meaning of the resurrection.

I have always found Brendan extremely generous with his gifts and with his time. He is always happy to do readings or make appearances for causes he holds dear, and, in relation to my own work with the homeless, I have found that he has a strong sense of social justice and has plenty to say about social issues. He has an ability to identify with the ordinary person, and especially with the person who has been uprooted and has had to leave home. Again, I suppose, this goes back to his Kerry roots and his sense of the importance of place. He has an empathy with the displaced, the emigrant, the lost, the homeless that I admire in someone who might so easily have become a distant academic or an elevated poetic personage removed from the realities of hardship and poverty and the ordinary, everyday struggle to make do, to get by, that is the lot of so many people in our society.

I love Brendan's poetry, but I also love his unpoeticness, his refusal to be aloof in the manner of poets, his delight in debunking the self-importance of poets and poetry, his simple ability to act the clown. I know that his doing voice-overs for ads offends some people (it's not the sort of thing poets are supposed to do), but it doesn't offend me; on the contrary, it makes me laugh, especially when I remember that he can't drive any car, much less a Toyota. He has a great sense of humour, and he has great wit and a sense of fun. He laughs a lot, and when I am reading his poetry, I can just see his smiling eyes and his round face and his dimple and sometimes I just roar laughing to myself at the thought of him. That is a great gift that he makes to us, the gift of laughter. He is able to laugh at himself, and he makes us laugh with him, at ourselves. He can see the fun in things as well as the deeper meaning, the mystery of our being and the mystery of the whole of creation.

Brendan Kennelly is a breath of fresh air, and Ireland is a better place for his being in it.

Brotherly Moments

My earliest memories of Brendan are of the songs he taught me, the money he gave me, and the football he played. I remember climbing into his bed in the morning, when we were both just awake, to listen to him singing 'The Croppy Boy'. I must have been no more than four or five years of age, but he taught me the air and words of that song. I couldn't understand many of the words: ''Twas a good thought, boy, to come here and shrive', or 'Upon yon river three tenders float'. What did 'shrive' mean? What did 'yon' mean? What did 'tenders' mean? He explained to me.

I was nine or ten when he went to work for the ESB. When he'd come home on holidays he'd give me money. He gave me half a crown once. It was a huge amount – you could buy nine 'Crunchies' with it.

He was a good footballer, skilful and stylish. I remember he wrote an article on the great Mick O'Connell, in later years, in which he tried to define the essence of that great man's attitude to the game. Mick O'Connell, Brendan wrote, concentrated on the skills of the game, applied his intelligence to it, exploited its potential to cultivate athletic grace and poise. Brendan would have found that article easy to write; he might have been writing about himself. Unlike Micko, however, Brendan never went near realising his full potential as a footballer. 'The Books' got in the way.

There were, nevertheless, some memorable moments. He had a great game in the 1953 North Kerry Championship Final when, playing alongside his brother Colm and John, he helped Ballylongford beat Ballydonoghue in an encounter still spoken about today. And I recall a Parish League game against Lenamore, Brendan playing poorly, failing miserably to realise the high expectations that were placed on him at this very local – and proportionally ferocious – level of competition. Mickeen Mulvihill, almost in tears, blaming him for what seemed certain, humiliating defeat at the hands of close neighbours. And then, with time almost up, Brendan scored a screamer of a goal to turn defeat into victory. Poor Frank Hanrahan, in goal for Lenamore, never saw the ball until it rested in the back of the net.

Above all, there was the All-Ireland Minor Final of 1954 when Kerry played Dublin. Brendan was at wing back. Kerry were two points up with a minute to go. Brendan fielded a ball in defence but was impeded (he says illegally!) in his clearance, which went just as far as an opponent, Vinny Bell! (How often that name has come up in conversation since!) Brendan tackled him and was adjudged (he says wrongfully!) to have fouled. From the resulting free Dublin scored a goal. Kerry had been beaten by a point with the last kick of the game.

In 1956 Brendan played junior football for Kerry. I remember the trip to Lismore where Brendan starred when Kerry beat Waterford in the Munster Final, and later to Pearse Stadium in Galway when the home team defeated Kerry in the All Ireland semi-final. At that time Brendan might have entertained realistic hopes of playing senior football for Kerry. He was just twenty years of age, and a gifted athlete. But – as the Kerry people would say – 'The Books' were his downfall.

When he returned to Trinity College for a second shot at an academic career, after a mercifully brief sojourn working as a clerk for the ESB, the football went by the board, and the gifted athlete became an outstanding student. There was an upstairs sitting-room in our house, beautifully furnished – and never used. 'The Big Room', we used to call it. During his holidays Brendan studied there for what seemed to me endless hours. Though I cannot give his exact timetable, I feel it must have involved up to twelve hours a day study. Perhaps from eight in the morning till nine at night, with breaks for just meals and brief walks. When, at night, he'd come to the pub, letting my over-worked mother off-duty, and chat and sing with the men of 'Bally'. He owes a great deal to those men – they probably saved his sanity, after the horrendous working schedule he had set himself. He delighted in their conversation, exchanging outrageous and bawdy banter with them, in tune with their wit, their humour, their graciousness:

> I've seen men in their innocence
> Untroubled by right and wrong,
> I close my eyes and see them
> Becoming song.
>   ('Living Ghosts')

He began to write, and much of what he wrote centered on the village he loved: 'The corner in Bally, a place of renown/It stands in the middle of our little town.'

When Patrick O'Connor emigrated to America he wrote a ballad lamenting his departure. When the local sergeant raided (successfully!) our pub for after-hours drinkers Brendan celebrated the event in mock-heroic style. Perhaps his most famous ballad is 'The Four They Left Behind', which recalled the events following the 1961

75

Munster Final when four Ballymen celebrated Kerry's victory, not wisely but too well. They missed the bus home:

> Four dauntless men were left behind, of hope they were bereft,
> Mike Tierney with his sandwich-bag and not a sandwich left,
> Bill Connor, Mairtineen, and Tom Keane made up the hopeless four,
> Said Bill, 'It seems to me we'll never see dear Bally anymore!'

However, a saviour emerged, who was to furnish our stranded supporters with the means to hire a taxi home:

> Four men alone, far, far from home and things looked far from well,
> But miracles will never cease; when they got to Scott's Hotel,
> They met a man with a heart of gold, his pocket was the same,
> And he lent the lads a fiver, though he didn't know their name.

Over thirty years later, you will still find Ballymen to recite this poem.

When I went to Dublin to train as a teacher I had reason to be grateful to Brendan. Aware, perhaps, of the loneliness which he, himself, suffered when he first went to Trinity as a student, he took me under his wing. I remember the first Sunday I spent in Dublin. Brendan met me under the clock in Westmoreland Street and took me to the cinema: *Lilies of the Field*, with Sidney Poitier. During my stay in St Patrick's Training College I never went short of cash. The Junior Lecturer in Trinity kept me well supplied. He gave me books, too. *Come Dance with Kitty Stobling* by Kavanagh. *The Girl with Green Eyes*, by O'Brien. Even *Ulysses*, which I never succeeded in reading completely. I was being educated, without knowing it.

Later, when I did a degree, through correspondence, with London University, it was Brendan who furnished me with all the books I required. Everything from *Beowulf* to Synge. All free of charge, which was a vital consideration for a young teacher with a mortgage and a family. He directed my studies over the phone from Bally to Dublin. He gave me invaluable advice and encouragement.

Though drink was becoming a dominant factor in his life, it never – remarkably – interfered with his writing. More and more, however, it was a factor. During his trips home at this time he usually stayed with me and my wife, Kate. Those were hilariously anarchic times. Picking him up at Tralee railway station. Hearing him before seeing him. Once, he placed two suitcases one on top of the other and wanted passengers to jump over them as they stepped off the train. Once, at the inevitable pub-stop on the way home, he poured water into his whiskey and then aggressively demanded that a giant of a man remove the water.

How to get him home without mishap! And then, when home

at last, he'd threaten the virtue of every lady he met, starting with Kate, who, the first time this happened, looked with alarm to me for protection. Later, when she got to know Brendan, she'd accuse him of being all threat and no performance. My children were delighted with his visits and would be inconsolable for days when he left. They were enthralled when he showed them the trick of cutting his thumb in half – and when he writhed in mock pain afterwards. Or when he pretended to eat turf. Or when he told them stories about the witch who lived in the chimney in Tarbert Island.

He hit Bally like a bomb at these times. The famous poet from Dublin was a bawdier talker and a harder drinker than the best of them. His great friend when he'd come home was Connie, a drinker like himself, but without the cash to indulge his thirst as Brendan did. When Brendan was at home Connie was never thirsty. When Brendan was away Connie was forever pestering me to know 'When is the Professor coming again?' Years later, when Brendan was on the dry, and on holidays in Ballybunion, he rang one morning. *Cromwell* was to open as a play in Dublin in a few weeks, and the producer wanted Brendan back at once to sort out some teething problems. Could I take him to the Limerick train immediately? On our way from Ballybunion to Limerick, and just outside Bally-longford Village, we saw Connie on the road.

Though in a hurry for the train, Brendan asked me to stop the car. A quick laugh with his old drink companion. A twenty pound note to help him over the morning's thirst. The last time he saw Connie.

During his alcoholic stays in my house he'd leave for the pub early in the morning and wouldn't return till nightfall – stoned out of his mind. Kate would have a meal ready for him. Once, he came home rather early, about four in the afternoon, with a total stranger. A drunk and hungry down-and-out. Kate sat them both to table to feed them. Brendan was cheerful, in great good humour. He was holding forth with authority on the virtues of drink, and being very disdainful of my lack of experience with alcohol. Meanwhile our stranger friend was attacking his meal as if it was the first time he had eaten in weeks. He began to stuff food into his mouth, gulping down big chunks. Then he began to choke. His face turned blue. The erstwhile authority on booze was transfixed with horror. 'Paddy – Kate – do something!' he wailed. Kate and I dragged this stranger (we never did get an introduction) to the lawn at the back of our house where, with the aid of a few strong thumps on the back from me, he disgorged his meal. Brendan was suitably chastened – for a while.

Brendan fought a great battle with the drink. To date he is winning that battle. Nowadays, at the height of his poetic powers, he works as demanding a schedule as he did as a young student in the 'Big Room'. He writes every day. Writing is a compulsive love for him. Recently he told me that if he were a condemned prisoner in a cell his last wish would be for pen and paper.

DECLAN KIBERD
Brendan Kennelly, Teacher

'Mol an óige agus tiocfaidh siad,' says an Irish proverb: 'Praise the young and they will come.' That was certainly the Kennelly philosophy of education. I recall sitting down for the first of his lectures of the Michaelmas term 1969 in the old Museum Building at Trinity College and introducing myself to the fellow perched next to me. I had hopes of striking up an early friendship with a classmate in a new, unfamiliar place. 'I'm not really one of your classmates,' the fellow whispered: 'I'm in Second Engineering.' Then he added with a conspiratorial wink: 'So are two or three others in this room.' Even in those far-off days Kennelly's fame as a platform lecturer had spread well beyond the confines of the English Department, though not yet to the outside world: he was one of those secrets which Trinity could keep to itself. The roll which he insisted on sending around each class, in a sly parody of collegiate pedantry, was really something of a joke: for there were always more people in the room than on the official departmental list.

Another poet-academic, W.H. Auden, once drily defined a professor as 'a man who talks in other people's sleep', but Kennelly was never in that number. Once, just once in all my pilgrimages to the Museum Building, I sat right in front of his lecture-stand and was astonished by the amount of physical energy he discharged in a fifty-minute performance – an energy which seemed to pass into all the bodies assembled in the room. The mood was passionate, intense, interrogative, committed, with no trace of irony or false sophistication. The urbanity and reticence on which so many Trinity people prided themselves played no part in his up front performance. At a time when most students made a point of seeming laid-back or even cool, he was all challenge and fire. It was a real change from the prevailing college styles, official and unofficial, and grounded in the conviction of his beloved William Blake that energy is eternal delight.

For a newly-arrived Junior Freshman, this was very heaven: a course on the Romantic poets in the autumn term. A quarter-century later, I still have my notes from those classes, scattered and cryptic though they be. They were written down after each session had ended, of course, because nothing annoyed Kennelly more than the sight of sixty bowed heads taking dictation. He often interrupted his own lectures to denounce sedulous transcribers: 'For

God's sake, if there's anything in this worth remembering, you'll remember it anyway – and what you don't need, you'll soon forget.' On one particularly bad day he savagely quoted Chesterton against the scratch of too many fountain pens: 'Ten thousand women said "we will not be dictated to", and promptly became stenographers.' Then he dared us to write that sentence down. He always hated those elements in the Irish educational system which induced rote-learning and deference to authorities in the exampassers' mode.

He was right, but there were so many *bon mots* in his lectures that you ached just to write a few of them down, if only to pass them on to your father or your girlfriend at the weekend. The ones I managed to jot down seem at this remove to tell as much about the speaker as about his subjects. On eccentricity: 'The eccentric is simply the man with a deeper than average apprehension of normality.' On those who settle in the suburbs: 'The image is of a corpse reclining into a coffin of complacency.' On paradox: 'It is by our inner contradictions that we become representative of struggling humanity.'

He praised Keats, according to my notes, for putting commonplace snatches of talk into his poems (much as he himself would later do to such effect in *Cromwell*). The great London lyricist 'was so pure and original that, inevitably, some of his poetry had to be trite'. This was also a quality to be noted in Kennelly: every so often, despite his formidable originality of mind, he would come out with some crashing platitude and proceed to enunciate it with all the innocent excitement of one who has just made an unprecedented breakthrough in the history of human thought. But such was his presence and charm that he could infuse even platitude with an unexpected intensity which made the familiar seem strange all over again. To hear him talk, sometimes, was to feel yourself in the company of another Adam at the naming of a new world, which was why he made such a brilliant explicator of the American Adams, from Whitman to Crane.

One of the central themes in the Romantic lectures was the danger of thrusting one's thoughts into a falsely premature coherence: in retrospect, this seems all the more valuable a point to have made at a time when various -isms were sweeping the campuses of the world, calling upon to the young to simplify themselves in the name of this or that vision. Praising Keats's ability to rest content with half-knowledge, Kennelly would tell his listeners that 'perplexity is the surest evidence that we have given close attention to a problem'. He went on to insist that all true acts of criticism are really forms of attention, the real word for which is 'prayer'.

One consequence of this which I noticed from the start was his deep love of quotation. The cynics (of whom there were, predictably, a few) would complain that the lectures, when you broke them down into their parts, were filled with long passages from the author under discussion. This was, in one sense, true. What such an analysis omitted, however, was the 'greeting of spirit' that is enacted when one mind meets another. Kennelly was not lacking in a sense of self – the very thought is risible – but his profound reading of Keats had taught him how to find an identity in external things by the simple fact of choosing what to identify with. It was the selectivity which bespoke identity: and so some of the lectures did indeed seem like long, loving passages from a marvellous edition of Keats's letters. Kennelly, for all his thumping energy and attitudinising, was truly humble in the service of those texts which he loved.

The mysticism of William Blake he described in a great phrase as 'a flight from the alone to the alone'. Praising his 'sensitivity to the total meaning of a word', he went on to cite his life as proof that 'complete sensitivity is self-destructive'. Blake 'saw the great in the little because he began always with the small, specific case' – the face in a London street that, fully studied, became a map of the war between the eighteenth century and the nineteenth; the feeling which (if persisted in) became an outright symbol.

Students of Kennelly's own poetry will probably see many links between these ideas and his own creative output. The same might be said of his year-long course for Junior Freshmen on criticism, for he tended to concentrate on the prefaces written by practising poets: Shelley, Dryden, Wordsworth, Dr Johnson, and so on. If this seemed to slight the more theoretical work of a Richards or a Leavis, it had the value of alerting students to the fact that someone like Patrick Kavanagh, far from being an untutored genius, was a profound and original thinker as well as a sophisticated, self-aware poet. In later years Kennelly himself took to writing short, evocative prefaces to his volumes, and I like to think that some of the ideas contained in them were first tried out on the eager faces in the Museum Building.

His characteristic treatment of students was praise, praise and more praise. On this matter Coleridge was his ultimate authority: 'who tells me what is wrong with a thing tells me nothing: who tells me what is right illuminates my day.' I wrote my own first essay for Kennelly on the *Biographia Literaria*, an audacious project for an eighteen-year-old: but it is a mark of the courage which he inspired in the young that not for a moment did I consider something more limited in scope. He not only gave his all as a teacher, but he taught his followers how to surpass themselves too.

Trinity in those years was a somewhat utopian place, an image of what Ireland might become in some future republic of the imagination. Walking across the cobblestones of Front Square from a lecture by Kennelly or a tutorial by Máirtín O Cadhain, a First Year might contemplate quite a range of fellow-students: medics and engineers from the Third World, historians and vets from Protestant Ulster, bohemian country house types from deepest England, and of course many young men and women from the schools of the Republic. Debates in the Hist. could be abrasive affairs at which members of the Republican Club, equipped with hurley-sticks, engaged with hardline loyalists, who had no compunction about speaking up. The ban by the Catholic archbishop of Dublin on attendance by his flock at Trinity was regretted by almost all, but it had the undeniable if unintended effect of ensuring that only the more independent-minded Catholics – like Brendan Kennelly – braved the Front Gate.

Nowadays, there are far fewer overseas students from either England or the Third World, and fewer still from the Protestant schools of the North; and when I return for a debate at the Hist., Trinity seems more like the UCD in which I have spent the past sixteen years. For me, however, the intensity of those undergraduate years found a final, unimpeachable symbol in the figure of Brendan Kennelly.

No platform lecturer whom I subsequently heard at Oxford could rival his passion, lucidity and wit. Some were more learned; many more wise; but none could send auditors scampering back to the library to fight over possession of the books which the lecturer had just been discussing. He remained in my mind always as a model of how the work of a lecturer should be done; and it was only when I faced the crowds in Theatre L at Belfield that the full immensity of his achievement became clear to me. Ireland has produced a lot of poets, of whom he is one of the truly interesting: but no country in any single generation produces more than a handful of inspired teachers. And, since the gift of true teaching is a matter of learning as well as instincts, I feel sure that some unsung man or woman back in Kerry in the 1940s was such as exemplar to him: for there is an apostolic succession in that craft too.

Sometimes, when I pass by Trinity's newly-whitened front, I am tempted to duck through the Front Gate and sneak into the back row of a Kennelly lecture to relive a past moment. But something always checks the instinct, saying, 'no, maybe my memories would be mocked.' And so I hurry on. Better to scan the fading notes, imagining the distant scene. For Kennelly was as good as the proverb. He praised the young – and they came.

PETER & MARGARET LEWIS

The Brendan Conquest: 1962 and All That

Climaxes came thick and fast during Brendan Kennelly's year at Leeds University (1962–63), but the literary climax was the launch of Brendan's poetry pamphlet *Green Townlands*. 'Launch' suggests liquid and splashing, and there was plenty of both at Whitelock's, the eighteenth-century tavern where the festivities took place. The gathering was small but the consumption of alcohol was on a Falstaffian scale. This was a necessary part of the proceedings if the blasphemous christening ceremony planned by Andy Gurr with the poet's complicity was to provide adequate relief for all those involved in the publication of the pamphlet.

Ladies were present [they certainly were! – *MBL*] at the imbibing part of the evening, but not at the highpoint in the Gents. This had nothing to do with either patriarchal domination or female modesty; the reasons were purely practical.

When all the men had reached bursting point, they led a sacrificial copy of *Green Townlands* out of Whitelock's for ritual blessing and purification in the primitive urinal – a wall with a drain. The main target to face the firing squad was 'Children's Hospital', the sentimental poem Andy Gurr had come to loathe during the production of the pamphlet by the School of English Bibliographic Press, which he ran. When all the weapons were correctly aimed at the condemned victim stretched out on the concrete floor of the Gents, the order to shoot was given, and the onslaught proceeded for well over a minute. *Green Townlands* was afloat. But isn't this what a book launch ought to be? During the performance a stranger entered the jakes, took one look and fled. If he'd known the pissing contest in Pope's *Dunciad*, which Andy had recently been lecturing on, he might have joined in the fun.

What did subsequent visitors that evening make of a slim volume of super-saturated poetry left stranded in the middle of the floor? Who could have guessed that thirty years later collectors were willing to pay up to £1,000 for a copy of *Green Townlands*? Had the Whitelock's cleaner rescued the urine-soaked masterpiece, just think what some American libraries would have forked out for this unique copy, signed by the author in such a personal way.

Green Townlands (to which Rudi Holzapfel also contributed two poems) was such a long time a-coming because it was produced as a research exercise in typography and printing by a tiny group of postgraduates working with Andy Gurr. Everyone involved was primarily engaged on other courses or research, Brendan himself on his doctoral thesis about Irish epic literature, to which he was later to contribute *Cromwell*, *The Book of Judas* and *Poetry My Arse*. The text of *Green Townlands* was hand-set letter by letter using composing sticks, as in the pre-machine era of typesetting. Experienced compositors can do this relatively quickly, but those involved were learning as they went, so the process was leisurely.

Brendan had been brought to Leeds from Trinity College, Dublin, by the charismatic Derry Jeffares, recently appointed to the Chair of English Literature. Yeats scholar, academic fixer of the highest order, and the man with the unforgettable laugh, Derry was rapidly transforming the School of English into a mini-United Nations with graduate students from every part of the world. Many writers and academics from just about everywhere dropped into Leeds at Derry's invitation, helping to generate an extraordinary multicultural milieu. The reverse of Derry's policy of 'bringing them in' was 'sending them out', packing Leeds graduates off to far-flung corners of the Commonwealth as part of his import-export trade. Among exports in the early 1960s was Tony Harrison, who went to Nigeria for a few years after reading Classics.

Also unusual at this time was Derry's interest in new creative writers, and Brendan benefited enormously from a year of contact with a wide range of poets and novelists, some on the staff, some visitors, and some still students, like Ken Smith and Norman Talbot. Peter Redgrove was the current Gregory Fellow in Poetry, Geoffrey Hill was a Lecturer, as was the Australian novelist and poet Randolph 'Mick' Stow, while Jon Silkin, a former Gregory Fellow, was engaged on research for his book on First World War poetry. The recently established Poetry Room, run by Geoffrey Hill, was a magnet for poets. Various student-run magazines, such as *Poetry & Audience*, appeared regularly, Silkin's *Stand* magazine was flourishing after its revival, while Poetry and Jazz sessions were enjoying a vogue in several pubs. Poetry was falling from the air.

Immersion in this literary environment was bound to affect a young poet like Brendan because of the sheer diversity of what was on offer. It was impossible to remain a Little Englander or a Little Irelander when confronted by writers from India, Australia, Canada, the Caribbean, New Zealand and several African countries, not to mention the US. It may have taken Brendan some time to absorb and digest the impact of Leeds, but his year there was a rite of passage.

If Leeds had an impact on Brendan, he certainly had an impact on Leeds. Derry had arranged for him to stay in Lyddon Hall, a small student residence very near the Victorian terrace housing the School of English, but Brendan found the atmosphere restrictive and claustrophobic, altogether too English. The playful advice he sometimes gave a fellow-Lyddonite when accompanied by a girl, 'Grab her by the arse,' was misinterpreted and deeply resented. In Dublin Brendan would have expected comparable women to reply in kind, giving at least as good as they got. In Leeds Brendan was actually accused of crudely insulting the flower of English womanhood. To many flowers of English womanhood, however, he proved irresistible, and faced with his twinkling eyes and flexed dimples, English reserve was quickly discarded. Arriving at one student party, Brendan approached a girl he hardly knew and said jokily, 'Get your coat. We're leaving.' To his astonishment she instantly obeyed and dragged him off. The rest is silence.

During the day Brendan could usually be found in the Research Room, one of two attic rooms in the now-demolished 1 Virginia Road, the three-storey headquarters of the School of English. Regular visitors to the Research Room included the poet Geoffrey Hill. This was an attraction of opposites: Geoffrey, the introverted, anguished perfectionist writing intensely concentrated poems slowly and with enormous care; Brendan, much more exuberant and carefree, tossing off poems with seeming effortlessness. Brendan would urge Geoffrey to let himself go and loosen up his writing. Sometimes Brendan would even pick Geoffrey up – no mean feat since he was a big man – and carry him round the Research Room shouting, 'You're constipated, Hill, you're constipated,' before depositing him in a heap on the floor. Brendan's frequently outrageous behaviour towards English people was in direct proportion to their inhibited restraint and inability to let their hair down. When we and Brendan took Geoffrey and his wife Nancy to dinner near Towton, site of the bloodiest battle ever fought on English soil (during the Wars of the Roses) and part of the inspiration for Geoffrey's sequence 'Funeral Music', Brendan was in exceptionally mischievous mood, entering the restaurant by climbing through the kitchen window and engaging the waiters in the most fanciful conversations about Irish dancing goats and other figments of his overflowing imagination. Geoffrey had to be physically restrained from racing back home.

Peter Redgrove, too, made periodic visits to the Research Room, one of which ended in a celebrated snowball fight outside 1 Virginia Road. The winter Brendan spent in Leeds was one of the most severe in living memory and there was no shortage of snow. After some teasing and ruderies from Brendan about the 'violent poet' image Peter was projecting at the time, the two poets resorted to inconsequential skirmishing with snowballs until Brendan approached Peter at a run with one of Brobdingnagian proportions. Peter hastily retreated round the corner of the house and was out of sight when Brendan launched his missile. Whether through luck or skill, Brendan succeeded in curving the mega-snowball round the corner in a way that a baseball pitcher or a fast swing bowler in cricket would have envied. A bull's eye. Peter's eye, in fact. He came back round the corner, snow covering his face, threatening retaliation as only 'a violent poet' could.

On most occasions, snow dropped from on high was, for Brendan, a form of flirtation with passing girls, who would be invited upstairs to see if they could melt his snow-white balls. In the evenings, the Research Room was the scene of forms of research other than the academic. Not the most comfortable of places, admittedly, but very private and no risk of being disturbed. Reports that queues of women students formed nightly on the stairs of 1 Virginia Road to partake of Brendan's 'midnight feats' were greatly exaggerated, but there is seldom smoke without fire. What is surprising is that the Research Room did not spontaneously combust.

Mocking pretentiousness became almost a mission for Brendan. In the 60s, Leeds University was intensely political and there was a great deal of socialist pomposity and jejune philosophising. The earnest self-righteousness of the English chattering classes has long been a source of mirth to others, especially the Irish, and Brendan set about deflating it with glee. He was often amazed at the gullibility of the English intelligentsia, naively prepared to believe just about anything they were told as long as it was told with a straight face. How, he argued, could they put such trust in something as conspicuously fickle and unreliable as words?

One of Brendan's most elaborate hoaxes, which a number of people swallowed hook, line and sinker, concerned D.H. Lawrence, then seen by liberal and leftist intellectuals as a heroic sexual liberator and a victim of oppressive bourgeois morality. This was not long after the *Lady Chatterley* trial. According to Brendan, Lawrence had stayed in his father's pub in County Kerry while working on a novel based on Irish mythology, notably the Black Bull of Kerry, and had abandoned the manuscript there because of his dissatisfaction with it. After providing details of the narrative, characters and symbolism, Brendan caused consternation when he speculated about the fate of 'that ould pile of papers'. Had they been lost or even used to light the fire? Devotees of Lawrence talked of setting out on a pilgrimage to recover the sacred text. We thought that it was only a matter of time before references to the lost manuscript began to appear in learned articles.

The only literary pilgrimage that Brendan himself joined was to Haworth, although without much sign of piety. In pursuit of the Brontës, he set off with a group of slow-moving Indians, an aristocratic Egyptian and the usual cross-section of our cosmopolitan English Department. By the time we reached Haworth, after a complicated bus journey involving several changes, Brendan was wound up as tight as a spring. While this largely Oriental cavalcade, saris fluttering, moved at a snail's pace up the steep streets leading to the Parsonage, Brendan dived in and out of shops like a wicked elf, demanding tinned Brontës or a pound of Brontës or four Brontës in a hurry. Talking Texan like John Wayne, he accosted an unsuspecting resident with a shopping bag: 'Say, old-timer, are we right for Wuthrin' Heights?' There was no doubt who deserved to sit in Branwell's chair when we finally got to *The Black Bull*. We did make it to the Museum, but Top Withens was way beyond the range of this group.

Brendan the entertainer was soon a familiar figure in Leeds, but Brendan the serious poet was always there beneath the fun and public gaiety. We laughed like mad at poems like 'Children's Hospital', hoping to teach him a lesson about cheap emotions. We urged him to beware of the familiar Irish traps: failing to escape from the clutches of Yeats and falling into the bog of facile lyricism. His mature work, in which he goes so deeply into the tragedy and triumphs of Irish history, shows how brilliantly he succeeded. Brendan undoubtedly missed Dublin and Ireland during his year out, but Leeds was good for him, at a formative point in his development, as it was for so many of us who were fortunate enough to be there during what now seems its golden age. Whether you were from Calcutta, Calgary or County Kerry, Leeds was a most challenging and stimulating place, and only the most reclusive could avoid having their political, moral, philosophical and literary assumptions questioned. Brendan may have done battle with posturing poseurs but he was deeply affected by the Leeds experience. His immediate response to all this was his second novel, *The Florentines* (1967). The long-term impact on his poetry is probably impossible to define, but none the less real for being intangible.

MICHAEL LONGLEY

A Can of Peas

(for Brendan Kennelly)

I open a can of peas and I open up
That factory, balancing on tons of pea-vines
And forking them out of the sky into machines,
Millions of peas on a white conveyor belt, sleepy
Eyes, surfacing from a vat sunk into the floor
A gigantic iron shopping-basket full of cans.

The only student-slave able for hard labour,
Kennelly helps me assemble my rusty bed
In a Nissen hut in the middle of vague England,
And create out of cardboard boxes a mattress,
There to pass out, aching, blistery, and waken
At dawn to a blackbird on the corrugated iron,

Kennelly's voice, long before children and wives
Helping me feel at home amid the productive
Cacophony, cans spiralling down from the roof –
Already the tubby, rollicking, broken Christ
Talking too much, drowning me in his hurlygush
Which makes the sound water makes over stones.

NELL McCAFFERTY

Meeting in Front Square, Trinity College

This fellow with the fabulous smile – it's a close run thing between him and Jack Nicholson – introduced himself to me in the cobbled quadrangle in Trinity College. It was in the 70s, I was relatively new to Dublin, and aware that the South was uncomfortable with the militant way things were developing in the North. He told me that he quoted my articles to his students as an example of morality and justice. He advised me never to weaken. He went on his way immediately. I stiffened my lonely backbone, wallowed in the compliment though I was not then aware of whom it came from, and have ever since checked my conscience against Brendan Kennelly's standards. He has had an effect on me that he never knew about – the gift and the unsung reward of a good and generous teacher – but also, ever since then, I too have made a point of stopping people who are sincerely trying and paid them tribute if it is due. And I go regularly to the dentist, in faint emulation of him and Jack Nicholson. Ah, such lads!

The Bold Collegian

I first met Brendan Kennelly when I went to Trinity College, Dublin, in the autumn of 1957. As a Kerryman, of course, the name Kennelly was well known to me as his brother Colm was, at that time, a celebrated member of the Kerry football team. Some years before we met, I had seen Brendan himself play, with some distinction, in the colours of the Kerry minors. It was, I suppose, not surprising then that Brendan and I should make our acquaintance through the Gaelic Football Club in Trinity and that I knew him as a friend and as a sportsman before I knew him as a poet, writer and academic that he was later to become. Even in those early days, however, Brendan was beginning to develop as a poet and while this may not have been recognised by your average corner forward his first book of poems, *Cast a Cold Eye*, published in 1959, set him on the road to literary recognition. I recall, too, that in his early days in Trinity, Brendan was a regular contributor to the College literary publication, *Icarus*, and that his loyal football friends bought that magazine only when a Kennelly poem appeared in its pages!

Whenever I look back on those college days, I think of Brendan first and foremost as a Kerryman. He loved football with a deep and passionate intensity not only because of the beautiful earthiness that could be found in playing that game but also, I believe, because he felt it to be part of the fabric of Kerry life and society. That sense of pride he felt in being a Kerryman was, a short time later, beautifully expressed in a 1964 poem, 'My Dark Fathers', when he proclaimed that he was 'come of Kerry clay and rock'. So he was and expressed it eloquently and wonderfully on the football field. Brendan's footballing days also call to mind that subtle and rather vicious sense of humour he so often displayed. This was a type of humour, it should be said, not always appreciated by the referee. One particular occasion springs to mind. The referee, in Brendan's view, was poor, inadequate and biased, so the irate Kennelly directed at that unfortunate official the worst insult any football referee could be given – 'And what part of Kilkenny do you come from?'

The Trinity Gaelic Football Club had many difficulties to overcome under Brendan's captaincy in the years between 1957 and 1961. True, one or two top class players were regular members of the team, including Kevin Heffernan of Dublin, the late Kevin Coffey of Kerry, and Sligo player Pat McHugh, but with as few as twelve footballers available on a regular basis it took all Brendan's ingenuity and persuasion to put fifteen players on to the pitch! Needless to say, Brendan succeeded and so many a footballer from the Dublin area who couldn't tell Red Square from Front Square had the honour of representing Trinity in those airy days. I remember an opponent once saying to me in all seriousness, 'I didn't know that Jock Haughey' – brother, I believe, of a future Taoiseach – 'was in Trinity.' Indeed he was not, nor was many another player who played for the University under Brendan's inspired and innovative captaincy.

As I was the only Protestant in the Trinity team of the late 50s, I recall that pre-match talks centred not only on football but occasionally on the Roman Catholic Church's ban on its members wishing to enter Trinity. Special dispensation had to be granted and many of our players had experienced some difficulty in getting their Bishop's permission. Not so with Brendan, however! He wrote to the Bishop of Kerry, sought his permission and received, so he told us, the following reply:

> Dear Brendan,
>
> Thank you for your letter and I hope you beat the stuffing [Brendan quoted His Lordship as using a more expressive word!] out of Cork in the Munster Championship next week.
>
> Yours sincerely,
>
> The Bishop of Kerry
>
> PS. It's all right about going to Trinity.(!)

I wouldn't wish to conclude my sporting reminiscences of Brendan Kennelly by leaving the impression that his love of football and of Kerry had a limiting and narrowing effect on his work and on his life. Brendan was always bigger and more Catholic than that, for after all, he wrote major works of *Cromwell* and *Judas*, two historical characters who might not be all that well respected in his native county and mine! In a strange way, Brendan's *Cromwell* brings me back to where I began – to Trinity's football pitch. On that pitch in those far off days, he expended much of his energy and expertise and, in difficult days, kept the club alive. He was player, captain and manager all rolled into one and I, for one, was not surprised that when he brought out Cromwell, in imagination, back into the present day, one of the roles he gave to that historical figure was that of a sportsman and as a leader of sporting men!

'Being a sporting chap, I'd really love to
Get behind one of the best teams in the land.
Manager, perhaps, of Drogheda United?'
        ('Manager, Perhaps?')

It may seem strange to many people now that Brendan did not play
a major part in College life while he was in Trinity. The fact that
he lived out of college may have had something to do with it, or
perhaps he was too engrossed in his new love affair with down
town Dublin City, where he was living, to have the time or the
inclination to display his wit and wisdom at debates in the Philosophical or Historical Societies. I'm glad, however, that from time
to time he was heard with much delight in Cumann Gaelach An
Choláiste. I recall, in 1958, when I was Reachtaire of the Cumann,
I invited Brendan and another Kerryman, Paddy Breen (we Kerrymen like to keep things in the family!), to represent the University
in an Inter-University debate in Irish. Brendan was, without doubt,
quite capable of debating in Irish, but on this occasion he decided
to impress the judges in an unusual way by speaking, apart from
using a few well chosen English words, almost entirely in the
French language! At the end of the performance he received a
standing ovation from all present for a wonderfully amusing
speech. However, the judges were somewhat unimpressed and
Cumann Gaelach Choláiste na Tríonóide finished last despite the
valiant effort of Paddy Breen!

Many years after those distant college days Brendan wrote a
poem entitled 'The Loud Men' which begins:

And how O God shall we learn to cope
With the loud men?

Those of us who knew Brendan in College would have smiled a
little as we read those words, remembering his larger than life
presence and his loud voice constantly expressing his great love
for life and his extraordinary enthusiasm for those profound and
genuine ideals that set mankind upon a high and noble round.
That loud voice that I heard leading his team, encouraging his
players, even criticising referees, is still, I am happy to say, heard
loud and clear by a wider and more diverse audience today. And
it is still, as it always was, a voice of reason and sanity, and of
deep understanding. Indeed, to quote Brendan himself, it is now,
as it was when I remember it first,

A passionate and gentle voice
Authentic as a patch of sunlight...

        ('A Passionate and Gentle Voice')

DOLORES MacKENNA

A Lap of Honour around the Cafeteria

At the end of the 1970s the Arts Council initiated a scheme which enabled Irish schools to invite established writers to come into the classroom to introduce their work to pupils and to encourage aspiring writers with their own efforts. One of the first poets to visit the school in which I teach was Brendan Kennelly. Such was the success of the experience that not only has it been repeated almost every year since, but it has become one of the highlights of the school calendar. 'Some things you remember forever,' Kennelly tells consumers in one of his radio advertisements. The young people who are fortunate enough to have attended one of the poet's school sessions would heartily agree.

Brendan Kennelly's reputation goes before him. Older students tell of the year he organised a laughing competition, of an impromptu song writing competition and of the time the poet accompanied a particularly successful competitor on what he deemed to be 'a lap of honour' around the cafeteria, an event which drew a crowd to the windows to see if the figure in full flight around the tables really were the eminent professor from Trinity College.

While the highjinks are long talked about and remembered with amusement and affection, so too are the more profound experiences of the day – the beauty of the poetry and the magic of its presentation, the breadth of discussion which follow and the depth of interest shown in the students' own work.

As a performer Kennelly is outstanding. Endowed with a wonderful voice and an excellent memory, he can command the attention of all – whether with one of the favourite poems of his audience, 'Poem from a Three Year Old', which asks the unanswerable questions which trouble all young people:

> And will the new young flowers die?
> And will the new young people die?
> And why?

Or with a poem such as 'The Pig-Killer' which deals with a topic not readily of interest to the urban teenager, but the sensuousness of the language soon compels them to appreciate the event:

> ...Tenderly his fingers move
> On the flabby neck, seeking the right spot
> For the knife. Finding it, he leans
> Nearer and nearer the waiting throat,

94

Expert fingers fondling flesh. Nodding then
To Gorman and Dineen, he raises the knife,
Begins to trace a line along the throat.
Slowly the line turns red, the first sign

Of blood appears, spreads shyly over the skin. The pig
Begins to scream. Fitzmaurice halts his blade
In the middle of the red line, lifts it slightly,
Plunges it eight inches deep...

Ever generous and reassuring Kennelly encourages even the shyest
students to come forward and recite their poems. Usually they begin
with some trepidation, but after several readings and some discreet
suggestions from the visitor for the deletion of a phrase here or the
addition of a word there, diffidence soon disappears to be replaced by
self-confidence and even pride in their work. Occasionally a student
may be so emboldened by the poet's response that some time later
she will send him a body of verse for assessment! Kennelly may be
a very busy man and she may never qualify as a contender for the
Nobel Prize for Literature but her efforts will always be greeted
with tremendous kindness and meticulous attention.

When Brendan Kennelly visits our school even the weariest
teachers look eagerly at their timetables to see if they can manage
to attend his session with the students. Not only do they enjoy his
poetry, but with the experienced eyes of professionals they marvel at
his ability to fire the imaginations of young people. For Kennelly
is the consummate teacher. He will seize upon the kernel of an
idea which has arisen in a poem and broaden it so that the young-
sters find themselves examining opinions they had always accepted
without question, but which they now see in a new light. A poem
entitled 'The Stones' tells of an old woman who is used by adults
as a scapegoat to frighten their children into obedience:

Worried mothers bawled her name
To call wild children from their games.

Not surprisingly, the children in the poem follow the example set
by their elders and see the harmless old lady as an object of irrational fear and treat her accordingly:

One child threw a stone,
Another did likewise.
Soon the little monsters
Were furiously stoning her
Whose name was fear.
When she fell bleeding to the ground,
Whimpering like a beaten pup,
Even then they didn't give up
But pelted her like mad.

From such a beginning a discussion emerges which leads the adolescents in the classroom to explore subjects such as the nature of prejudice and of justice. Words are found to articulate the most difficult concepts – even by those who might normally be regarded as the least able students. Somehow the debate moves from the "easy" notion of other people's prejudice to the thornier question of the audience's own bias. With all the honesty of youth, views are aired – some consoling, some amusing, some alarming. The confined world of the classroom is seen to be a microcosm of the greater world.

Confronting the problems of society and our attitudes to them leads us to confront ourselves. Kennelly does this in his own poetry. In *The Book of Judas* he writes of the biblical Judas and also of Judas, the betrayer, who is in everyone:

> You'll meet me at a twist in yourself
> Which you must not confuse with a bend in the road...
> Because there, at that twist in yourself, sin
> Is born again, the days can bless and damn,
> You will swallow the old dark, the old light,
> Meeting me in yourself, soon; but not yet.
> ('Twist')

But as *The Book of Judas* itself illustrates, the dark side of human nature can produce works of great beauty. Young people in particular appreciate this. Conscious of their developing selves – the angst as well as the excitement of their lives – they quite naturally express themselves in poetry. Most of it goes unread by anybody except themselves. Brendan Kennelly's visit allows them to share their insights, searchings and yearnings with him and with their peers. Their teachers are often both surprised and delighted by the quality of the work which emerges on these occasions.

In his Introduction to *Breathing Spaces* (1992), a selection of his early poetry, Kennelly says:

> There's always the hope that education and learning, like law and justice, may occasionally coincide.

At a time when education seems to be more and more examination oriented, with both pupils and teachers driven by the necessity of obtaining ever increasing numbers of 'points' in the Leaving Certificate, this ideal fusion of education and learning is often difficult to maintain in our day-to-day teaching. A visit by Brendan Kennelly to our classrooms allows those of us who are lucky enough to be there an opportunity to enjoy just that experience. We are heartened by the knowledge that in this case

> The learning goes on forever.
> ('The Learning')

96

HUGO MacNEILL

Deeds of Glory and Voices in the Head

It was a warm spring evening during my final undergraduate year in Trinity College. Having two years of Foundation Scholarship to run I wanted to spend one of these studying Anglo-Irish literature before going on to Oxford. 'You should meet Kennelly,' advised my friend, the ever sage professor Trevor West, 'to make sure he realises you're genuine and it's not just an excuse to stay to play rugby!' Since I was (genuine) and it wasn't (an excuse), West and I duly made our way to O'Neill's hostelry in Suffolk Street where the great man had arranged an audience. There ensued the first of many wonderful evenings in Brendan Kennelly's company. Conversation flowed back and forth and showed no sings of easing when the good gentlemen of O'Neills were required to fulfil their legal obligations in bringing down the shutters. Since all three of us were living in college we adjourned to that waterfall of books that constitutes Brendan's rooms. Journals, students' essays, piles of publications old and new competed for space and attention across the floors and tables. The banter between West and Kennelly was now in full and irreverent flow. Having travelled through the realms of politics, Irish literary history and various aspects of college life their argument came to alight on a dispute as to which of them was the better sportsman. Each advanced their case, citing various feats of glory whilst demolishing the supposed achievements of the other in the most eloquent and merciless fashion. Being both such products of the twentieth century their dispute could not be left entirely to theoretical or abstract speculation; empirical verification was required.

   Notwithstanding the lateness of the hour (it being now past 2 a.m.) we hauled ourselves from deep armchairs, ventured out into the shadows of Front Square and pointed ourselves in the direction of the College Park. The square was all darkness and sleep except for an occasional light where some soul jousted with the frontiers of knowledge. Little did they or the great minds of the slumbering academic and student body realise that one of the most memorable sporting events of Trinity's long history was about to take place. It was to prove somewhat ironic that one of the participants, T.T. West, was later to chronicle Trinity's sporting history in his book *The Bold Collegians*, published on the occasion of the college's quatercentenary in 1992. No matter how often the reader leafs

97

backwards and forwards through West's tome will he find mention of what was about to ensue. A pair of curious eyes peered from the doorway of house number 38 as our merry band passed the billiard table lawns of New Square. The sounds of late night revelry drifted from high windows of 35 on the far side of the Quad.

Adrenaline was pumping furiously in the veins of the two latter day Collegians as we entered the College Park. The lights of Nassau Street glimmered in the distance. The absence of the moon and the presence of thick low clouds made the green playing field ever darker than normal but we could make out the running track. 'Choose your distance West,' barked Kennelly. West paused, stroking his chin somewhat nervously as he deliberated as to whether longer or shorter would better suit his cause. In typical fashion, he chose neither. '400 metres it is,' he replied, 'a complete lap of the track.' Jackets were removed, sleeves rolled up and both crouched over the starting line, their eyebrows almost joined in concentration, tilting forward in uncertain readiness. 'On your marks, get set' and both men bolted from the traps in the direction of the law library. The Ballinacurra greyhound, as West was dubbed by Kennelly (due to his wiry build and his East Cork origins) took an early lead as they went into the first bend, Brendan following with arms and legs pumping like a threshing machine out of control. Into the back straight parallel to Nassau Street and Brendan's Gaelic football pedigree came to the fore as he caught and then passed the then Senator and Professor of Mathematics. Some daylight, so to speak, was emerging between the two as they neared the final bend. West, fearing the worst, realised that the darkness could be his only saviour. Perhaps the story of the famous Grand National run in fog came to mind when the jockey of the second placed horse, could not believe his eyes as a horse in front of him passed the winning post in triumph completing his second circuit of Aintree, he swearing that he had never been passed.

As Kennelly's pumping arms pulled further away West played his last desperate card, veering sharply to the left, thus bisecting most of the final bend. For most periods of the year this might have been a successful, if highly unethical, strategy. Darkness was now, however, to play both friend and foe. Being at the height of the cricket season the practice nets stood fully but invisibly upright. Into the netting at full tilt came Senator West, uprooting the pegs and bringing the entire structure down on top of him. Kennelly sped down the home straight, his arms raised in triumph, his head thrown back in wild laughter. This was my introduction to the remarkable Brendan Kennelly.

So many themes and incidents compete as one tries to capture what it is that makes Brendan so special. Though sounding incredibly trite I think it is the emphasis he puts on each person as an individual. Let me try to explain what I mean. In our daily lives a number of powerful forces constantly push us towards categorisation and generalisation. The formidable array of new technologies, of e-mail to voice-mail to Internet, seek to summarise, to condense, to attain precision and unambiguous expression which may capture much of the skeleton but lose most of the flesh. Our attention spans are shortened; bullet points, soundbites and instant opinions are the norms of "communication". Within this formidable flow of information, attention to the richness and diversity of the individual can easily get lost.

Brendan as both teacher and citizen treats each person as an individual. To him everyone has a particular and indeed unique story to tell and he has a genuine enthusiasm for discovering it. In class he would draw out the person sitting quietly at the back as more insistent voices would offer and reoffer their opinions. As that person became more involved Brendan would encourage, gently probe and challenge, always listening carefully, until he or she was fully engaged with new-found confidence and enthusiasm.

This gift showed itself in other related ways. I recall a dark drab winter's Monday night. I was waiting for Brendan in O'Neill's. Perhaps half a dozen people were in the bar. In the corner an elderly woman sat reading the evening newspaper. At the far end of the counter sat a man sipping his pint, passing an occasional word to a grey-haired man sitting at a nearby table. The barman leant over the pumps, chatting to a regular who was particularly incensed by some recent parking regulations. It struck me as a pretty unremarkable scene. Brendan suddenly swept in, nodding in recognition to each as he joined me at my table. 'See her?' whispered Brendan nodding at the woman in the corner. 'She paints lovely but slightly mad pictures.' 'And your man,' he continued arching his ear towards the figure at the end of the bar, 'tells absolutely wonderful stories. The fellow at the far end' (whom I hadn't noticed), 'has gone through some tough times but has a voice like an angel.'

I looked around again, seeing them all in a new light. It was clear that Brendan didn't know them particularly well. However, it was also clear that on some occasion he had sat down and by talking, and particularly by listening, had entered into what Yeats called 'the labyrinth of another person's being'. His way naturally celebrates what makes people different and distinct and sees categorisation as both insulting and as a missed opportunity.

His response goes further than listening when required. On another occasion we were sitting at the same table when into the bar came a man in his fifties carrying a holdall and a big Dunnes Stores bag. His appearance and demeanour suggested that his fortunes had known better times. He ordered a drink and sat down at the next table.

'How's it going?' asked Brendan.

'Not too bad,' came the reply.

It turned out that he was off on the night boat to Liverpool, having been out of work for a while and his marriage recently having broken up. Brendan enquired as to the fact that he didn't have a coat. 'No,' he replied. Brendan slipped out, returned to his rooms and came back twenty minutes later with his own overcoat which he duly presented to the soon-to-be emigrant. He paused a moment, opened his holdall and gave Brendan an old transistor radio, insisting that he couldn't accept the coat without giving something in return. Brendan accepted it, mindful not just of the man's practical needs but of his dignity. Such instinctive and impulsive generosity was typical.

Some years ago, after seeing a hypnotist show, I remember reading about what was called the 'critical censor'. For all I know, this may be a spurious scientific concept but I found it an interesting way of looking at thugs. At the risk of simplification it was described as that faculty which screens suggestions and tells us whether they make sense or not. For example, if someone suggests walking down the street naked this censor tells us it's not a great idea. Apparently hypnotism relaxes this critical censor. It can work in other related ways. When we pass a beggar in the street our primary human impulse is to help but then some cousin of the critical censor intervenes, rationalising that they should be working or the money will go on drink, etc, etc. Brendan seems to circumvent this crudely described critical censor, trusting his initial instincts and impulses. Does this mean he gets taken advantage of? Probably. Does it mean that he taps into a much richer vein of people? Definitely. He is known as a remarkable talker, praise which is certainly merited. But, as I said, he is also a remarkable listener.

He loves all sports and is typically articulate on its poetry, drama and passion. We used to meet up on the Monday nights after rugby internationals when I was at Trinity. I loved hearing the stories of the people he met on his walk to and from Lansdowne Road and various points en route. He was no passive spectator. In 1988, when Ireland played Wales, he went to the game with my uncle. Each time Paul Thorburn, the Welsh full back, lined up a kick at goal, Brendan would rise and dramatically recite various ancient Gaelic curses, roaring with laughter and punching the air as the kick sailed wide. It was a remarkable tour de force according to those who watched it. As the game went on, each time the referee's whistle sounded a Welsh penalty, that entire section of the stand turned expectantly to the bard, clapping wildly at each new offering. Unfortunately he was 'short taken' at a crucial moment late on and was sadly in the Gents as Thorburn, unimpeded by divine or pagan intervention, sent the ball high through the posts for the winning score.

Brendan tells it as he sees it. There is a wonderful passage in Tom Wolfe's *Bonfire of the Vanities* when the book's main character Sherman McCoy is with his parents and children at their luxurious house in Long Island. He is one of Wall Street's giants, a so-called 'master of the universe'. 'But what do you actually do Daddy?' asked his puzzled son. 'I'm a bond trader,' he replied citing the name of his firm, remarks which would have been sufficient to have listeners nodding respectfully at cocktail party or golf club. No further explanations would be needed. But children are more direct. 'But what does that mean?' his son continued. Sherman unsuccessfully tried to explain, tying himself in knots on seeking to put in plain and simple terms what was so important about this job which accorded him such wealth and prestige. I have seen Brendan play the role of the child in talking to people who have lofty pretensions about their importance in either the social, business, academic or political world. 'What does that actually mean?' he would ask as someone self-consciously declaimed on their activities in a manner, the purpose of which was to demonstrate their own importance. 'Someone once said to me, "Kennelly, you write like a child",' he recounted to me once and continued: 'I replied that it was the nicest compliment anyone had ever paid me. For some reason he was totally flummoxed.'

Brendan cuts straight to the centre of things. In a recent lecture in London, President Mary Robinson spoke on various themes relating to the role of the University at the present time. She quoted from a distinguished former President of Yale University who spoke of our teachers becoming 'voices in our heads'. I had often thought of Brendan in this way, as his is one of the voices which I have heard in my head most often over the years. And do you know what? It is always worth listening to.

Voices from Tralee

1

ÅP: 'Excuse me, does the name Brendan Kennelly mean anything to you?'
Woman 1: 'Of course, poet from Kerry.'
ÅP: 'Do you know any of his work?'
Woman 1: 'No, but I saw him once, in Killarney. I was at a wedding, he was walking down the street, and a friend of mine, she knows everything about him, she loves all his stuff, so she ran up and asked for his autograph, and he was talking just to her.'
ÅP: 'Have you seen him anywhere else?'
Woman 1: 'Absolutely, I've seen him on television, he's famous all around Ireland.'
ÅP: 'Thank you very much.'

2

ÅP: 'Do you know who Brendan Kennelly is?'
Man 1: 'He's a writer, everybody knows him in one way or another, he goes to every opening of everything.'
ÅP: 'Have you read any of his work?'
Man 1: 'I've heard some of his work, but I've never really…It's not my style, I've no interest. I can appreciate what he does, but personally it's not my field of interest, at all.'
ÅP: 'OK, thanks.'

3

ÅP: 'Have you heard of Brendan Kennelly?'
Man 2: 'No, not really.'
ÅP: 'Not at all?'
Man 2: 'Kind of, yes.'
ÅP: 'How?'
Man 2: A writer, or a musician, I'm not sure, I've heard of him, but…'
ÅP: 'Thank you.'

4

ÅP: 'Does the name Brendan Kennelly ring a bell?'
Woman 2: 'A poet.'
ÅP: 'Anything else?'
Woman 2: 'I know that Mary Robinson is a great fan of his. I like his poetry, I don't know it too well, but the little bit I know I like.'
ÅP: 'What do you like?'
Woman 2: 'I suppose he has the gift of bending the contemporary issues into a lyricism that is…but I don't know his poetry very well. He's a modern Irish person, he's also making a political contribution to Irish society, he's another voice that says things that only poets can say.'
ÅP: 'OK, thank you.'

5

ÅP: 'Does the name Brendan Kennelly mean anything to you?'
Woman 3: 'It does to me. He's a writer and he's also from Kerry.'
ÅP: 'Have you read any of his work?'
Woman 3: 'No. Well, maybe one or two poems when I was young and foolish.'
ÅP: 'How have you heard of him?'
Woman 3: 'Seen him on the TV, listening to the radio. He's a lovely chap, a great sense of humour, a ladies man, a real gentleman.'
ÅP: 'OK, thanks.'

6

ÅP: 'Have you heard of Brendan Kennelly?'
Man 3: 'Poet, yes, but I haven't read anything, just what I would have heard on the radio. I wouldn't read poetry.'
ÅP: 'Do you know of him only as a poet?'
Man 3: 'No, I've just seen him on television chat-shows, he does advertising also for certain cars.'
ÅP: 'Do you have any opinion about him?'
Man 3: 'He's good, he's funny, he's funny at times, always a smile in his face, very jolly.'
ÅP: 'OK, thanks.'

7

ÅP: 'Do you recognise the name Brendan Kennelly?'
Man 4: 'Brendan Kenneally? I do, yeah.'
ÅP: 'How?'

Man 4: 'Is that the Brendan Kenneally who is on hungerstrike in Britain?'

ÅP: 'I think that's Kelly.'

Man 4: 'Oh, what did you say? Brendan Kenneally? No, but I know of a Tim Kennelly, a footballer. I'm Lenihan, myself. But I don't know Brendan, no.'

ÅP: 'Thanks.'

8

ÅP: 'Does the name Brendan Kennelly sound familiar to you?'

Woman 4: 'It does, yes.'

ÅP: 'Why?'

Woman 4: 'A writer. He comes from Kerry, isn't that right? His brother is a priest in Kerry as well. He actually works in Trinity. And he's got grey hair, and he's going bald!'

ÅP: 'Any other comments?'

Woman 4: 'I've seen several interviews on the Gay Byrne Show, the *Late Late Show*, he's often a guest, he's into all the current affairs, very outspoken. He's very liberal, incredibly liberal, really, that's brilliant, that's a breath of fresh air to the country, just what we need.'

ÅP: 'Thank you for answering.'

9

ÅP: 'Brendan Kennelly, do you know who he is?'

Woman 5: 'Yeah.'

ÅP: 'Tell me.'

Woman 5: 'On the radio. He's a singer.'

ÅP: 'Singer? Have you heard anything else about him?'

Woman 5: 'No.'

ÅP: 'OK, thanks.'

10

ÅP: 'Have you heard of Brendan Kennelly?'

Man 5: 'Brendan Kennelly, yea, he's a poet, writer, yes.'

ÅP: 'Have you read his work?'

Man 5: 'Not really, no, no. I've never seen him in person, just on television, on the chat-shows.'

ÅP: 'Do you agree with what he's saying?'

Man 5: 'I'm indifferent to him.'

ÅP: 'Thank you.'

11

ÅP: 'Does the name Brendan Kennelly mean anything to you?'
Man 5: 'It does, of course, yes, poet and a very good scholar, he's from Listowel, but he's Dublin-based now, I'd imagine.'
ÅP: 'Are you familiar with any of his poetry, or other activities?'
Man 5: 'I've just seen him on television, on several occasions, but I don't know much more about him, really, just what I've read in the papers. He writes very good articles. A very nice type of man, I feel if I met him personally he'd be very nice. He always has a smile in his face, he's that way, he gets through to you, kind of thing. He has a great way with words.'
ÅP: 'Do you disagree with anything he does?'
Man 5: 'He probably drinks too much, but you can't blame him for that, can you?'
ÅP: 'Thank you for your time.'

12

ÅP: 'Are you familiar with Brendan Kennelly?'
Woman 6: 'Poet and author. I listen to him a good bit, I think he's very good. We'd go to anywhere he is just to hear him, we would, when he's in Kerry. Some things he says are very nice, he's very natural, down to earth, that's about it.'
ÅP: 'Thanks.'

T. P. MAHONY

The Most Gifted of Men,
or, Poet, Go-Cart and Craic

It is a wonder of the man himself that I couldn't tell you when I first met Brendan Kennelly. I feel I have known him all my life. Though my first contact with the family may well have been through face-to-face meetings with his great footballing brother, Colm, on the Gaelic fields of Ireland. Brendan's most enduring and most endearing properties are his humility, his love of life, his love of people and his love of the truth. Add to these what could be considered personal self-effacement and you begin to know Brendan Kennelly. Who, for instance, would agree to lend his uniquely melodic voice to a TV go-cart commercial, advertising Toyota vehicles, and at the same time willingly publicly pronounce his inability to drive a car!

Since first I knew him, meetings with Brendan Kennelly – and, thankfully, there have been many – are moments of inspiration and delight. Delight at meeting a poet of such truly international repute and yet one so willing to understate his great self.

I remember some years ago meeting a young teacher who was due to face her first encounter with Professor Kennelly at a poetry workshop. She was almost ashamed to admit that she had never heard of him, knew none of his poems and did not even know what he looked like. Yet, on driving to the first night of the week-long course, she remembered years previously receiving a gift of a book called *Cromwell*, which she read in one quick night, and quickly discarded it, hating every brutal line of it. But having arrived at the course she found it impossible to remain indifferent to Kennelly's company. She was not sure if it was the magic of his voice, the attractive twinkle of his eyes, the disarming openness of the man or the sheer beauty of his poetry. She admitted that it suddenly made her feel alive. Like others, she felt challenged by a whole host of feelings on each of those evening readings and sharings. What stood out for her was the warmth and passion of the man who told his class that there was so 'little left worth hiding'; the honesty of a person who saw his poetry as a 'sharable moment of light' and the humility of a poet who never took himself too seriously and who acknowledged, in 'The Gift', that poetry for him was a 'gift that took him unawares' and he 'accepted it'.

Brendan Kennelly is shocking but not obscene; intimidating but not loud or aggressive; affirming but not patronising; and time spent in his company challenges you to 'open the doors of rooms that are never fully known', encourages you to take the risk and in doing so to 'Discover the buried good,/Be vulnerably new' ('Good Souls, to Survive').

We were, therefore, 'vulnerably new' when we asked Brendan Kennelly to play a pivotal role in some advertising programmes. Some people looking in at us from the outside might wonder why we chose to ask him.

But we are a 100% Irish owned company and have always been. In the past, we have strongly identified ourselves with things Irish, and in certain years over 25% of our advertising budget carried our advertising messages in Irish.

In expanding upon this marketing stance, what better way to subliminally identify our roots than by asking Brendan to play the central role? That he did is a great credit to him, and the stylish manner in which he did it undoubtedly lead to great public reaction and added immense value to our marketing programmes.

What makes for genius? What is a truly great work of art, piece of music, poem? Who knows? What I can say with certainty is that Brendan Kennelly's poetry speaks to me, moves me, warms me and touches countless others who are acquainted with his writings. Perhaps it is the immediacy of his writings which, as he says, find a voice in the 'byways, laneways, backyards and nooks and crannies of self' which appeal to so many. Or perhaps it is the freshness of his poetry, the newness of image and phrase that yet are rooted in the traditional and loveliness of Irish life. And which touches the reader. For we all know what he means when he tells us, in 'The Brightest of All', that 'the sun/Strode like All Ireland Victory into the room'.

While the poetry is also shocking, upsetting, irreverent, it is full of humour, full of love and full of variety. Kennelly tells us in the Preface to *The Book of Judas* that,

> in the society we have created it is very difficult to give your full, sustained attention to anything and anybody for long, that we are compelled to half-do a lot of things, to half-live our lives, half-dream our dreams, half-love our loves…

This is an accusation that cannot be levelled at a poet who loves so completely: his poetry is full of love, love of women and mankind, love of God, love of life. His passion for life and living allows him to celebrate all aspects of life, to celebrate the uncelebrated courage of the unsung.

Kennelly merits serious attention for, in a world which guards its words cautiously, he is not afraid to speak out with shocking openness, for he knows that this is 'A Time for Voices', and he prays, in 'May the Silence Break', to let 'the silence break/And melt into words that speak/Of pain and heartache/And the hurt that is hard to bear/In the world out here/Where love continues to fight with fear...' (*A Kind of Trust*, 1975). *The Book of Judas* is a tough read. It's crude, cruel and bitter in places. But Kennelly's voice can also be gentle and full of gratitude for the gift he accepted so warm-heartedly, the gift of poetry that is his. It is this gift that he offers when he writes in 'A Giving':

> I take the mystery of giving in my hands
> And pass it on to you.
> I give thanks
> To the giver of images...

It is difficult, perhaps impossible, not to take Brendan Kennelly seriously as a warmhearted, generous person and as a poet who is always ready to laugh at himself and who perhaps does not merit himself too highly.

> Sure even that fat little bollox
> Out in Ballylongford, Kennelly,
> Is half-able to write
> With a drop o' Listowel water in his belly.
> ('Moloney Enters into a Dialogue Concerning the Listowel Water Supply,' *Moloney Up and At It*, 1984)

Kerry has given this great little country of ours many of its most innate beauties. From its wondrous mountains, lakes and coastline to the silky skills of Mikey Sheehy. But it has given us little better than Brendan Kennelly.

I would dedicate Brendan Kennelly's own words to himself:

The Missionary

> Dear Souls, I am here on behalf of God.
> My mind is made of His light.
> I'm ready to shred my flesh, shed my blood
> Doing His work among you. It
> Is clear that all your gods must go
> Back into the darkness from which they came.
> I tell you this because I know.
> You, your women and children will know the same.
> Pray, O my brothers, for humility
> And courage to surrender to the true.
> Each man is a star, his soul is bright
> As anything the heavens have to show.
> Heaven's brightness flows to you from me.
> And on behalf of God I say, that's right.

GERALDINE MANGAN

The Boss!

Brendan Kennelly, bawdy bard, Fellow of Trinity College and Professor of Modern Literature, agony uncle, friend, father, grandfather, father-in-law, broadcaster, novelist, poet, dramatist, media personality, heart-throb, colleague, friend, sports enthusiast – in short a human being with a heart as big as a whale and an intellect to match.

These are just some of the words which come to mind when I attempt to "describe" Professor Kennelly whom I first met when I came to Trinity College as a temporary secretary in the Summer of 1976. Many's the time I've asked myself what makes him "tick". Rightly or wrongly, I feel that the bottom line in all he says and does is his search for the truth. If there is one thing that he abhors it is hypocrisy in any form. This is one thing 'the cute Kerry hoor' cannot stand and like a highly trained sniffer dog he always detects it and has nothing but contempt for the perpetrator. One would need to get up very early to con him. In fact, I'd go so far as to say that it is a near impossibility for he reads people and situations like an open book, such are his extraordinary powers of observation.

A Kerryman from the top of his head to the tips of his toes, he has adopted Dublin, a city which he loves dearly and in which he feels very much at home. What is its appeal for him? High on the list is the Dubliner's ready wit, his interest and curiosity in all that is going on and above all his colourful turn of phrase. No better person than the true Dub to get to the core of the matter, to see things as they really are and, what is more, to speak his mind. And these are all attributes which Prof, as I like to call him, admires. Dublin the city, it, too, holds a very special place in his affections. Nothing pleases him more than to walk through the city early in the morning, especially on Sundays, when all is relatively peaceful and quiet and to savour its own very particular atmosphere and beauty.

And what of Kennelly the educator? Herein, I think, lies at least in part one of the reasons why he is so very much in demand. Having worked for Professor Kennelly for just under twenty years, I have been fortunate enough to "observe" him in action on many fronts. Dare I say that his success and popularity as a teacher/educator lie in the fact that he has never strayed from the real meaning of the word 'educate', to lead. Education in the truest sense of the word is a sharing of knowledge and experience, a voyage of discovery, never, never an imposition of ideas or beliefs but an invitation to think, to explore, to seek to understand more fully both people and ideas. Behind that jovial, humorous front is a depth, a seriousness, an earnestness to understand and, I believe, to be understood. Behind the jocose, rollicking exterior lie a sensitivity and a concern for others born from no small degree of suffering experienced in his own life and an awareness and an acknowledgement of the isolation and solitude which are part of the human condition. How else can one explain the endless stream of people – students, worried parents, radio and television producers, listeners, viewers, teachers, nuns, priests – the list is endless – wanting to talk to him? In this age of technology, of instant information, what people want and need more than ever is communication in the deepest sense of the word, real communcation between individuals, a non-judgmental ear, a sharing of experience. How often in talking through problems or worries with a *real* listener, does one come to see things in a somewhat different light, from a different vantage point? Here Professor Kennelly excels. In short, he gives people hope, a sense of belief in themselves and in their own worth.

If I have a criticism of Prof, it is that he is a very bad hand at saying 'no'. There is only a limit to which any one person can go in their efforts to be all things to all men, even with the best will in the world. I often think of a phrase I first heard uttered many years ago by an eminent Jesuit, an ecumenist in every sense of the word: 'There is no use being so heavenly minded that you are no earthly good.'

Bureaucracy is a "non-word" as far as Professor Kennelly is concerned. Rules are made to be broken. In so far as they are a means to an end well and good, but once they become ends in themselves or, worse still, obstacles or deterrents – too bad. One must have the courage of one's convictions, be true to oneself, have faith in oneself, speak out.

Professor Kennelly can and does frequently cause "mayhem" but mayhem of an uplifting kind! He can reduce a semi-civilised, quiet office to uproar in a few minutes with his cryptic, often trenchant comments and remarks. He does not like to see people take themselves too seriously. Laugh and the world laughs with you; cry and you cry alone. Unconventional he certainly is, the antithesis of the absent-minded professor! Indeed, he has a remarkable memory for detail. Seldom if ever does he forget or fail to keep an appointment or commitment.

One lesson I have learned from working with Professor Kennelly is how inconsiderate we can all be in our demands on others. The price of fame and notoriety is loss of one's privacy, a fact which is borne out by the unending inquisition and dissection of those in the public eye. People need time and space for themselves (there are only so many hours in the day), so please let us have respect for one another.

Last but by no means least, I would say that Prof's sensitivity, his compassion, his awareness of others, are all borne of a very deep and real faith. And I have no doubt that it is this faith which is the source of his appeal, the reason why he touches the lives of so many from the highest to the lowest in the land. Foreigner or local, old man, woman or child, prisoner or prelate, unskilled worker or professional, amateur or academic. It matters not a whit. Prof is the same with them all. He is truly a man for all seasons.

Long life to you, Prof. Upya Boya!

The Gesture and Its Cost

My Father Perceived as a Vision of St Francis
(for Brendan Kennelly)

It was the piebald horse in next door's garden
frightened me out of a dream
with her dawn whinny. I was back
in the boxroom of the house,
my brother's room now,
full of ties and sweaters and secrets.
Bottles chinked on the doorstep,
the first bus pulled up to the stop.
The rest of the house slept

except for my father. I heard
him rake the ash from the grate,
plug in the kettle, hum a snatch of a tune.
Then he unlocked the back door
and stepped out into the garden.

Autumn was nearly done, the first frost
whitened the slates of the estate.
He was older than I had reckoned,
his hair completely silver,
and for the first time I saw the stoop
of his shoulder, saw that
his leg was stiff. What's he at?
So early and still stars in the west?

They came then: birds
of every size, shape, colour; they came
from the hedges and shrubs,
from eaves and garden sheds,
from the industrial estate, outlying fields,
from Dubber Cross they came
and the ditches of the North Road.
The garden was a pandemonium
when my father threw up his hands
and tossed the crumbs to the air. The sun

cleared O'Reilly's chimney
and he was suddenly radiant,
a perfect vision of St Francis,
made whole, made young again,
in a Finglas garden.

I wrote down that poem one rainy evening a few years back after running into Brendan Kennelly crossing Front Square in Trinity College. The shoulders of his overcoat were soaked (a slate blue number he wore for years), and he blended in, grained in, against the shiny cobbles and the ponderous stone. He invoked that poem, or provoked it, from me. It was nothing he said, I am sure, more the gesture he might have made, throwing open his arms to welcome the world, and he may not even have made that gesture, though he has always the air of having made it about him. A generous gesture. The one I give to my father in the poem when he throws up his hands and tosses the crumbs to the air. It was a melancholy night and the rain was dripping down his face; *vulnerable* was the word I carried home with me and which hovered around my tongue as I wrote 'My Father Perceived as a Vision of St Francis'.

I was asked once where I'd 'locate' Kennelly. I'd have to find him first, I said, wanting to disrupt the ranking game my conversee was angling for. Like the nun reputed to have run up to him with *You're my Toy-ota Boy, Brendan* when that ad hit the airwaves, I am unashamedly partisan. On the pinnacle of Parnassus I'd put him, though I suspect he'd be bored stupid within the week and find his way back down to his true habitat in language – that zone where the anarchic energies of the street push head on at the academy's walls. And threaten to pull him asunder, I suspect. For if there's anything I've learned from Kennelly it's about the human cost of the work. That everything in poetry is gifted as both curse and blessing.

He taught me at Trinity where I was an undergraduate from 1972 to 1977. What I hold in mind from his lectures – and to be honest, I hold little in mind having been frequently not in my right mind in those days – what he communicated, was the suffered human life behind the text, that poetry came from the inarticulate reaches of the wounded heart and had little to do with fluency and certainty. That its greatest achievements were built on the failure of language, and that failure itself would be the constant bedfellow of the poet. And especially that the text exists as a memory of the human voice that was once raised against chaos and can be recreated again and again from the text for those who have the inclination to listen. He seemed to be telling us that there was nothing new to be said but we had to keep making poems over and over, generation after generation, lest we forget that we are human. Lest we forget. Not that there was anything gloomy about those lectures, and they come back to me now wreathed in laughter and as something I looked forward to. They were worth getting out of bed for, and at certain phases of my life as a student there wasn't much I'd say that about. As my granny had it – do you have to wear black in that place? Is it an education you're getting or notions?

I think he saved my life once. I'd dropped out of the university and gone rambling and had been working in an apple orchard in Denmark. I was called home suddenly when my mother took bad. She died in Blanchardstown Hospital while I was being harassed at Heathrow by two CID louts who took my apple picking apparel for terrorist's garb. Her last words to me five or so months before were 'You'll never see me alive again.' Mine to her were 'I don't care.' Things had got to that stage. She was killing herself with drink and there was nothing I could do. I came back into an emotional hell. I didn't want to be in Dublin, or Ireland, next nor near the place. I was in bits. I had just gone in to the college to meet a friend soon after her funeral and was waiting under the arch. Kennelly passed by. 'Welcome home,' he said. I was stunned that anyone in that institution had even noticed I was away, and I'm sure he knew nothing of my troubles, nor even my name; probably he just knew my face from around, for the classes were very large and I wouldn't have spoken with him personally. But it unlocked something in me, the gesture of welcome in a city that was doing my head in.

When I began to publish poems in the 80s with Beaver Row Press he was a great encourager – and I use the word with its Latin ghost, *cor*, the heart, at the root of it. He gave me heart. He opened the doors of compassion. As an exemplar he showed me the working life of the poet/teacher and guided me to whatever path holds me now to its direction. Once when I'd come back to Dublin after yet another ramble and faced the bleakness of the dole and *nowhere* to live, he suggested I sign up to work under the Arts Council's Writer in the Prisons Scheme. I was discovering for myself that to teach is really to learn, something he's been saying for years. He's been criticised for being too prolific: I don't understand. He's hard-working. The extraordinary achievement of *Cromwell*, our own fifth gospel that is *The Book of Judas*, and one of our greatest feminist texts, *Medea*, are a harvest from the years of opening to the voices of his country by putting so much out in the public domain. I'd say even the Toyota ad fed his curiosity about the human soul – and sure how else would he meet the models for some of his most scurrilous characters? Not that he needs defence, being a founder of the Fuck the Begrudgers School of Poetry.

The first poem of his I ever read was 'Yes'. I was walking Howth Head with Kevin Page and he'd copied it out from some newspaper or journal, I think. We'd come up through the rhododendron gardens and he was raving about this poem he'd happened across. I was thinking more of Molly Bloom's affirmatives not far from where we stood. I read 'Yes' and wasn't impressed – too simple I opined. Too simplistic. We argued all the way down to the harbour. Now if Brendan had been a Chinese sage, or had an unpronounceable East European name, I'd probably have thought it was brilliant. I was seventeen and the only living poet I had read was Thomas Kinsella because he was on the Leaving. I was easily dazzled by cleverality and polysyllabics. But 'Yes' got in under my skin, and my own ridiculing of it comes back over the years to haunt me. Cynicism was a coping strategy and poetry was elsewhere and exotic. I hunted down the poem recently and found –

> We have all
> Thought what it must be like
> Never to grow old,
> The dreams of our elders have mythic endurance
> Though their hearts are stilled
> But the only agelessness
> Is yes.
> I am always beginning to appreciate
> The agony from which it is born.

What did I know? It's taken me twenty years to understand the gesture and the cost.

JANE O'LEARY

The Art of Listening

I first met Brendan Kennelly (although it is unlikely he will remember this) in the staff room of Swarthmore College, Pennsylvania, just over twenty years ago. I was lecturing at Swarthmore while completing doctoral work in music at Princeton University, prior to my move from America to Ireland. Since then, my creative pursuits have been closely entwined with Brendan's poetic musings. Over the years, I have enjoyed watching him watching people and distilling the surface complications of life. His poetry has 'entered' me and inspired me; I wish to thank him for both his way with words and his insights into the creative process and into life itself.

As I look back over the poems which relate specifically to musical creations of mine, there are a few recurring motives which appeal to me and also seem to be central to Brendan's output. My earliest references to his poetry were, logically, direct settings of texts for vocal renditions. In later years, texts took on a more philosophical reference point for abstract music and appeared only in titles and programme notes – preparatory material for the listener, reflecting thoughts which occupied my mind during the process of creation.

My first setting of Brendan's poetry was a work for choir and flute, written for the then RTE Singers and performed at the Dublin Festival of Twentieth Century Music in 1976. In setting the poem, 'Begin', I was immediately struck by the sheer optimism it expressed and by the poet's joy in simple everyday things which are often overlooked. Underlying the text is a faith in the goodness of life, its continuity and renewal:

> Though we live in a world that thinks of ending,
> That always seems about to give in,
> Something that will not acknowledge conclusion
> Insists that we forever begin.
>
> ('Begin', *Good Souls to Survive*, 1967)

Equally important, there was a musical flow to the words which immediately caught my ear and which made my task as a composer quite easy – the words simply demanded their musical setting!

As I got to know Brendan better, he was always generous with his poems and encouraging to me. He did not hold them to be precious, but wanted them to be shared and sent out into the

116

world, to reach people in as many ways as possible. I have been continually drawn to the sound of Brendan's poetry – it is often best read aloud and very special when read by himself. I recall hearing him read at the Project Arts Centre in the mid-70s in a performance generated by modern dance interpretations of his poetry. The visual element is as strongly present in his work as the musical.

One of the pieces recited (and danced) on that occasion was 'Lightning' from the collection *The Voices* (1973). In 1977, I selected three poems from that collection and set them for soprano, oboe and piano. This was first performed at the Dublin Festival in 1978 as 'Three Voices: Lightning, Peace, Grass'.

I liked the idea of objects speaking, the voices drawing the listener into another world. This is what I want my music to do – to challenge the listener to hear the silences of the world rather than assault his/her sensibilities with clamorous sounds.

Each of the three 'voices' I worked with spoke of a quiet place which is inside us all:

> My deepest nature is quiet and private.
>> ('Lightning')

> I am
> Beyond all things
> Even your dream
> Of me.
>> ('Peace', *The Voices*, 1973)

Closely allied to this inner peace is a positive outlook – life is bigger than any of us, and it is good – if we allow it to be.

> I will change you if you let me.
> I will.
>> ('Peace')

Some years later, in 1990, I returned to this same collection of poems for the unlikely choice of 'Silence' as a text for a choral setting. The choir was Cantairí Óga Átha Cliath, an excellent choir of secondary school girls. The work was called 'To Listen and To Trust', a phrase from the poem 'Silence'. The music also included a beautiful poem by Moya Cannon, 'Listening Clay'. The power of silence has always intrigued Brendan: in 'Peace' he talks of peace as being always present, 'my influence/Breathes in the dog's throat', and in 'Silence' he refers to the difficulty we face in confronting the absence of sound. In today's world silence seems to be

> A shadow on the ground,
> Someone always in the wings
> Or just outside the room...

As a musician, I recognise the power of silence. We must listen rather than ignore...

> Come towards me...
> I wait for you...

In today's noisy world, where life becomes louder and more aggressive all the time, I search for this inner peace. Brendan's words say powerfully what I can only attempt to say through a quietly reflective music.

In his 'Poem from a Three Year Old', Brendan takes on another voice, that of a small child. This is one of my favourites and has found its way into my music over the course of several years. Its attraction lies in its blend of simplicity and depth, innocence and perception. At the time of setting this poem for soprano, flute and clarinet (1976) I was writing instrumental music which was highly structured. It was a relief to turn to this poem and find the vocal line writing itself instinctively. The persistent questioning of the child relating people to flowers easily transfers to a musical motif. Here, as in the poems of *The Voices*, Brendan acts as the instrument through which another voice speaks. It is this gift of receptivity and humility which I feel is essential to creativity of any sort.

> And will the people die?...
> And why?

In 1982, I returned to the world of choral music and wrote a set of six songs on poems from the Irish which Brendan had published under the title *A Drinking Cup* (1970). This time Brendan is allowing ancient voices to be recreated through him. The starkness of these poems combined with a beautiful imagery and again a musical flow of words created music with little effort on my part. A number of these poems have also been set to music by Nicola LeFanu and I know that for her also the words wrote their own music. One of the poems that speaks particularly powerfully ponders the same question as our 'three-year old':

> Each night, morning, on land, sea,
> I realise again and again
> I must die. But why? Or how?
> Or when?

> ('Uncertainty', *Love of Ireland*, 1989)

The phrase 'I must die' repeats itself in my song, as a recurring drone, while the short and terse questions are carefully placed against it.

'Poem from a Three Year Old' has stayed vividly in my mind over many years. As I worked on a set of orchestral miniatures in 1986, I began to view the work as a series of opening gestures unfolding one by one, like flowers opening their petals. Lines from the poem kept speaking to me as I wrote: 'the petals fall' had to be the title of my work and formulated the ending of the variations.

> ...and do the petals fall from people too...

The poetic words were now speaking through my music in a more removed way and a new phase to my relationship with Brendan's poetry began. Moving from direct transcription of spoken words to sung words, I now began to draw on Brendan's philosophy and its relationship to my own creativity.

In 'The Story', Brendan again speaks through the voice of another – this time a story which has died in today's society. He speaks of the

> ...emptiness
> Spread by the story's death...
> That once lived on lips
> Like starlings startled from a tree,
> Exploding in a sky of revelation,
> Deliberate and free.

In this case, the imagery connecting the spoken flow of words to the dramatic outburst of birds from a tree captured my imagination. I wanted to tell my story in music with this same energy and compulsion, the combination of deliberate and free being essential to my method. All of these ideas were with me as I worked on music for strings in 1988, eventually titled 'sky of revelation'. A quotation from the poem is an essential part of my programme note.

Brendan has said that for him poetry is 'an entering into the lives of things and people, dreams and events, images and mindtides' (*Breathing Spaces*). It is precisely this ability of his to 'enter into' that I admire. It is, I agree, essential to creativity to lose yourself in the process and let other voices speak. Two of my more recent works for piano relate to this concept.

As I deal with the sound world, one of my obsessions has always been with the after-effects of sound...what happens after a note has been struck? This is different from the silence which brings it into being. Nowhere is the resonance more obvious than

119

in the after-effects of a bell. As I worked on a piano piece in 1989, I thought of bell-like resonances and played with the subtle changes that work on such lingering sounds, drawing the listener in more and more as the sounds fade. Imagine my delight and surprise in discovering yet again, as I browsed through Brendan's poems, that my thoughts were perfectly mirrored in his words. How could I resist setting the mood for my listeners with phrases from one of the versions of 'Entering':

> To be locked outside the image
> Is to lose the legends
> Resonant in the air
> When the bells have stopped ringing.

The work was titled 'When the bells have stopped ringing' and was premiered at Kilkenny Arts Festival in 1989.

Similarly, having completed a piano piece for the Dublin International Piano Competition in 1994, I knew exactly my feelings about the process of creation, but could not think how to convey this in words. While titles of musical compositions may seem irrelevant, I feel they provide the listener with important preparation for an otherwise confusing journey. Browsing again, this time on a train between Galway and Dublin, I remember shouting with pleasure as I stumbled across words which expressed just how this music had come to me and knew that the title of my piece would be 'From the crest of a green wave':

> It was taken from the crest of a green wave...
> I took it, soon it was gone...
> It is not a music that will live alone.
>   ('A Music')

As we struggle to create new voices, we must reflect upon those that are already there, speaking to us, and we must always listen. For this lesson, I want to thank Brendan and to tell him that he need never doubt his musical ear. His poems not only open doors and windows, but sing.

NORMA SHINE

The Great in Our Midst

I don't know Brendan Kennelly personally, but some time ago I won a trip to London because of him. The *Social & Personal* magazine ran a competition for a luxury weekend in the Four Seasons Hotel in Hyde Park, London. In order to win, one had to choose a famous person to share this weekend with – I chose Brendan and won the prize. To compete, one had to say in a limited number of words, with whom one would like to spend the weekend and why! Well, I chose Brendan, and the following 'Limerick' won the prize – thank you, Brendan!

> He looks like he needs heaps of cuddles,
> (that is all I mean!)
> Brendan is a charming being,
> Classics for breakfast,
> Theatre for tea.
> We'd have a ball, he and me.

Included in the prize was a copy of Brendan's latest work, *The Trojan Women*. I call him by his first name because somehow 'Mr Kennelly' doesn't seem to fit. Some years ago, I read a book of his poems, *Breathing Spaces*, and ever since then I've been a fan. He's courageous because poetry is so self-disclosing. He's a witty poet but much of it has also serious thought. He sets free and lights up the often unexposed happenings and moments in everyday life and brings to life that which is sometimes so brief it can pass by unnoticed. Most of his work has this warm human ring to it that strikes a chord with most people, but as the saying goes, 'there are exceptions to every rule', and in my opinion the exception this time is his latest poetry book, *Poetry My Arse*, where the language is disappointingly crude; it's definitely not for the fainthearted.

When we were in Secondary School, our year produced a school magazine, and on the opening page was the following anonymous poem, 'Embers', which reminds me of Brendan and his work:

> Say something before we go. Interest's a key
> To unlock the cell of self so we can walk
> In the air awhile. We are all poisoned, then why
> Be so aloof? Talk kindles a glow
> To see by. Even a shout may crack the roof.
> Let in a star...say something before we go.

I love to see him on television or hear him reading. His voice is captivating. He radiates this combination of vulnerability and strength which makes him so attractive. Hearing him on radio or television he can make anyone feel good about themselves. It's as if when you see him or hear him he generates a feeling of hope, and his smile, well, that's a poem in itself!

He has an accessibility which breaks down any barrier between him and the ordinary person on the street. Some months ago I met him quite by accident, and told him about winning the trip to London. He's a very warm person to meet, one of 'the Greats in our midst'.

I'd like to finish by quoting from my favourite poem of his, 'The Good', because, I think, here Brendan's own words go some way to explain his huge appeal:

> Always, they retain a kind of youth,
> The vulnerable grace of any bird in flight,
> Content to be itself...

NOTES ON CONTRIBUTORS

Åke Persson was born in Sweden in 1959. He edited Brendan Kennelly's critical essays, *Journey into Joy: Selected Prose*, and has published extensively on Kennelly. A graduate of the University of Karlstad, Sweden, and Trinity College, Dublin, he is currently completing his PhD thesis on Kennelly at the University of Gothenburg. He has also studied literatures in English at the University of Hull and at the University of British Columbia, Vancouver. Between 1986 and 1993 he taught Swedish and Scandinavian Studies at Trinity College, and is now Head of the English Department at Sigtuna International College of the Humanities, Sweden.

Bono hails from Dublin. Singer with the group U2, he is one of the most prominent and popular personalities in contemporary Ireland.

Gay Byrne has for more than 30 years been Ireland's outstanding broadcaster, being the producer and presenter of the immensely popular television chat-show the *Late Late Show* and presenter of the equally popular radio programme the *Gay Byrne Show*. Born in Dublin, he was educated at the Christian Brothers' School, Synge Street, Dublin, and on leaving school he went into insurance, cinema management, car hire and advertising before moving to broadcasting for Radio Éireann (now RTE) in 1958. He began his television career with Granada TV in Manchester and later moved to London with BBC 2. He has received several awards for his work, including the Jacobs Award for Broadcasting in 1963, 1970, 1976, 1978 and 1982. He also holds an Honorary Doctorate from Trinity College, Dublin. He is married to harpist and singer Kathleen Watkins, and they have two daughters.

John G. Cooney is a Consultant Psychiatrist. He is a former Associate Medical Director of St Patrick's Hospital, Dublin, and former Director of the Alcohol Treatment Programme at the same hospital, as well as lecturer in the Department of Psychiatry, Trinity College, Dublin. Publications include *Under the Weather: Alcohol Abuse* and *Alcoholism: How to Cope*.

Katie Donovan was born in 1962 and spent her early youth on a farm in Co. Wexford. She studied at Trinity College, Dublin, and at the University of California at Berkeley. She spent 1987-88 teaching English in Hungary and now lives in Dublin where she writes for the *Irish Times*. Author of *Irish Women Writers: Marginalised by Whom?* she published her first collection of poetry, *Watermelon Man*, in 1993, and has read her poetry in Ireland, England, Belgium and the United States. She is co-editor, with Brendan Kennelly and A. Norman Jeffares, of the best-selling anthology, *Ireland's Women: Writings Past and Present*, and edited *Dublines*, an anthology about Dublin, with Kennelly.

Harry Ferguson is not a Kerryman. He worked as a lecturer in Trinity College, Dublin, for five years, and is now Senior Lecturer at the Department of Applied Social Studies, University College, Cork. He is also a frequent contributor to the main Irish newspapers.

Allen Figgis is a former publisher and is presently Administrator of Christ Church Cathedral, Dublin.

Paddy Finnegan was born on a small farm in Kilkerrin, Ballinasloe, Co. Galway. He was educated at the Franciscan Brothers' School and St Jarlath's College, Tuam, and later studied literature and history at University College, Dublin. He has worked in various departments of the Public Service and joined the *Big Issue* enterprise on its inception in Ireland in 1994. He has had one collection of poems published, *Dactyl Distillations*, and is presently working on a second collection, to be entitled *Cosmic Perambulations*.

Liam Gorman is Joint Director of three MSc (Management) Programmes for senior managers and public servants run jointly by the Irish Management Institute and Trinity College, Dublin. He took his degrees at University College, Dublin, including a Ph.D. in psychology. He has written several books on management in Ireland. His recent publications and research are on corporate culture, the future of work and the relationship of Irish subsidiaries to their parent companies in multinational corporations.

Jack Hanna has worked as a teacher, telephone operator and journalist. He is the father of Davoren Hanna, a young handicapped poet who died in July 1994. He is at present writing a memoir of his life with Davoren and with Davoren's mother, Brighid Woods Hanna, who died in July 1990.

Marial Hannon is a graduate of Product Design from Galway Regional Technical College, and completed postgraduate studies in Arts Administration at University College, Dublin, and Cultural Project Management at Fondation Marcel Hicter, Brussels. She is now Education and Cultural Development Officer with Shannon Heritage and works on the research and development of contemporary arts-based pan-European multimedia programmes. Currently she is completing research for the establishment of the 'International Life-STORY Centre of Europe' project.

Charles J. Haughey was born in 1925 and educated at Scoil Mhuire, Marino, St Joseph's, Fairview, University College, Dublin, and Kings Inns, Dublin. He was Leader of the Fianna Fáil Party in 1979-92, and Taoiseach of Ireland for many years during that period: 1979-81, 1982, 1987-89, 1989-92. He was a Member of Dáil Éireann (Irish Parliament) in 1957-92, and Minister for Justice for two periods, 1960-61 and 1961-64; Minister for Agriculture, 1964-66; Minister for Finance, 1966-70, and Minister for Health and Social Welfare, 1977-79. He holds several Honorary Doctorates: Dublin City University, National University of Ireland, Université Blaise-Pascal (France), and University of Notre Dame (USA).

Sarah Hunt is 17 years old and currently preparing for her Leaving Certificate in June 1996.

Derry Jeffares was born in Dublin and now lives in Fife Ness in Scotland. He has held several professorships – among them at Leeds University – and published and edited many books, the most recent ones including *A History of Anglo-Irish Literature*, *W.B. Yeats: A New Biography*, *Yeats: The Love Poems*, and *Jonathan Swift: Selected Poems*. Together with Brendan Kennelly he edited *Joycechoyce*, and with Kennelly and Katie Donovan, *Ireland's Women: Writings Past and Present*.

John B. Keane is one of Ireland's most prolific, popular and critically acclaimed writers. He was born in 1928 in Listowel, Co. Kerry, where he now lives. Since the play *Sive* in 1959, he has written a vast number of plays, among them *Sharon's Grave*, *The Year of the Hiker*, *The Field* (also made into a highly acclaimed film, starring, among others, Richard Harris), *Big Maggie*, *Moll*, and *The Chastitute*. He has also published many collections of short stories, humorous essays and letters, as well as novels, most notably *The Bodhran-Makers* and *Durango*. Holding Honorary Doctorates from Trinity College, Dublin, and Marymount Manhattan College, New York, he has been given several awards, including the *Sunday Tribune* Award for Literature (1986), the *Sunday Independent* Special Arts Award (1986) and the American-Irish Award for Literature (1988).

Sister Stanislaus Kennedy of Focus Ireland was born in Co. Kerry but now lives in Dublin. Outspoken on social issues, she is dedicated to the development of new initiatives to combat and alleviate homelessness.

Paddy Kennelly was born in Ballylongford, Co. Kerry. He was educated at St Brendan's College, Killarney, and later at St Patrick's Training College, Drumcondra, Dublin. He is a National School teacher by profession and the author of a novel, *Sausages for Tuesday*, as well as a text-book for secondary schools, *Pathways*.

Declan Kiberd was born in Dublin in 1951. He took a degree in English and Irish at Trinity College, Dublin, and he holds a doctorate from Oxford University. Among his numerous books are *Synge and the Irish Language*, *Men and Feminism in Modern Literature* and *Idir Dhá Chultúr*. He writes regularly in Irish newspapers, has prepared literary scripts for the BBC, and is a former director of the Yeats International Summer School. He has lectured on Irish literature and culture in more than 20 countries, taught Irish at Trinity College, Dublin, and been a lecturer in English at University College, Dublin, for the last sixteen years. He is married with three children.

Peter & Margaret Lewis were postgraduate students at Leeds University from 1962 to 1964 and got to know Brendan Kennelly at that time. Peter is now Reader in English at the University of Durham and has written books on John Gay, Henry Fielding, John le Carré and Eric Ambler. Margaret works in the Public Relations Office of Newcastle University and has written the authorised biography of Ngaio Marsh as well as a study of Ellis Peters. They established Flambard Press in Newcastle upon Tyne in 1991 and are committed to publishing new and neglected writers, particularly from the north of England.

Michael Longley, regarded as one of Ireland's foremost poets, was born in Belfast in 1939 and studied at Trinity College, Dublin. He recently retired from the Arts Council of Northern Ireland where he was Combined Arts Director. Collections include *Poems 1963-1983*, *Gorse Fires* (which won the 1991 Whitbread Poetry Award) and *The Ghost Orchid*. He is married to critic Edna Longley and they have three children.

Nell McCafferty was born in Derry in 1944. After taking a degree at Queen's University, Belfast, and travelling extensively, she returned to Derry, where she joined the Labour Party and the Civil Rights Movement. She now lives in Dublin, where she works as a journalist, mainly for the *Sunday Tribune*, for which she has covered the situation in former Yugoslavia. Publications include *The Best of Nell*, *Goodnight Sisters*, *A Woman to Blame: The Kerry Babies Case*, *Peggy Deery: A Derry Family at War*, and *Nell on the North: War, Peace and the People*.

127

Reverend John McCarthy was ordained as a Priest in the Church of Ireland in 1963. He was Rector of Enniskillen and Dean of the Diocese of Clogher and resigned from the Church of Ireland in 1994.

Dolores MacKenna teaches in Dublin at Loreto Secondary School, Foxrock. She has written a number of textbooks for schools, and is a critic and occasional broadcaster. Currently she is writing a literary biography of the novelist and short story writer, William Trevor.

Hugo MacNeill studied at Trinity College, Dublin, between 1978 and 1982. A Foundation Scholar in Economics, he also took a Diploma in Anglo-Irish Literature. Being one of Ireland's most prominent rugby players, he played for Ireland 37 times between 1981 and 1988 and played in Triple Crown winning teams 1982 and 1985. He has an MLitt in Economics from St Edmund Hall, University of Oxford, and is now working as Investment Banker for Goldman Sachs in London.

T.P. Mahony is Chairman of Toyota Ireland. After a Cork North Monastery education, he entered the Civil Service but moved to industry and was involved in setting up the Shannon Duty Free mail order scheme for the US market. Other experience includes spells with Irish Ropes and Wavin Pipes before moving into the motor industry. He first became involved with Toyota in 1973. As a recognition of his contribution to the economy and to arts and culture, he has received Honorary Doctorates from Dublin City University and University College, Cork.

Geraldine Mangan was born and educated in Dublin. She has worked as Secretary in the Department of English, Trinity College, Dublin, since 1976.

Paula Meehan is a Dublin-born poet and now considered as one of Ireland's most interesting and exciting poets. Her most recent work includes the two critically acclaimed collections, *The Man who was Marked by Winter* and *Pillow Talk*, and the selection *Mysteries of the Home*. She writes for the theatre, for TEAM, Ireland's premier theatre-in-education company, and has collaborated with contemporary dance companies, musicians and visual artists. She has twice been nominated for the *Irish Times* Poetry Award, and in 1995 received the Martin Toonder Award for Literature.

Éimear O'Connor (cover) was born in 1965 in Dublin, where she currently lives. A full-time professional artist, she has exhibited widely in Ireland and the United States, and is gaining increasing international acclaim. Apart from painting, she also works with video, soundtracks, glass, photography, and set design (most recently for Channel 4).

Jane O'Leary is a full-time composer, also active in the performance and promotion of contemporary music as Director of the chamber ensemble Concorde, and Chairperson of the Contemporary Music Centre, Dublin. Born in Connecticut, she has been living in Ireland since 1972 and is based in Galway.

Norma Shine comes from Athlone, Co. Westmeath, and works as a secretary in Dublin.